ASPIRES
TO
LOFTY HEIGHTS

ASPIRES
TO
LOFTY HEIGHTS

Go and make disciples of all nations

ROSS MCCALLUM JONES

To order additional copies of this book, contact:
Xlibris
1-800-455-039
www.Xlibris.com.au
Orders@Xlibris.com.au
777624

CONTENTS

PART 4 REAPING THE HARVEST

To my dear late wife Joy,
a great homemaker,
wife, mother,
discerning counsellor,
and a godly co-worker in our ministry.

FAITH MISSIONARIES

In the latter half of the 19th century a vibrant missionary force developed and focused on the unreached; the tribes, languages, peoples and nations who had never heard of Jesus Christ. It had its origins with the founding of the China Inland Mission by Hudson Taylor in 1865. Over forty such missions followed including the Sudan Interior Mission (1893), later known as Serving in Mission or simply SIM. These independent faith missions became a significant feature of world evangelism whose glorious achievements, according to Herbert Kane, are stranger than fiction and more marvelous than miracles. Faith missions have been associated with conservative evangelicalism. They believe the Bible to be the inspired word of God, Jesus Christ to be the Son of God, God himself, and in the indwelling Holy Spirit, who empowers those who recognize their own shortcomings. They believe that Jesus died on the cross for the sins of mankind, dying in their place and taking the punishment for their sins. They believe Jesus is coming again, visibly, so that everyone will see him, and that he will reign on earth for one-thousand years; the promised Messiah who will judge the living and the dead. They also believe in the necessity of sinners being born again of the Spirit of God, and being clothed in the righteousness of Christ, thus becoming God's children, having a personal knowledge of Him, and living a godly life while depending on him.

Faith missions derive their name, not from the fact that they have great faith in God, but because the financial policy of faith missions often guarantees no set income for its missionaries. Faith missionaries raise their own support, and in some cases that support has been pooled in a spirit of sharing. Risking life and limb to bring the gospel to the lost is not taken lightly. Many of today's missionaries serve in countries with a high security risk. They are motivated by a clear picture of hell and of lost souls entering the eternal torment of hellfire. Their beliefs and practices may seem strange to some, but to them, these are the normal and clear teachings of the Bible. Earlier missionary recruits were without higher education, getting their training from Bible Institutes. Moody Bible Institute in the US stands out as a training ground for faith missionaries, having prepared thousands of people for service in faith missions. I spent two years in preparation for missionary service at Melbourne Bible Institute in Armadale in 1966-67. As well as studying the usual subjects: Old Testament, New Testament, Theology, Church History and Ethics, I began learning Greek and Hebrew, the original languages of the Bible.

Evangelism has always been paramount for faith missionaries and newer innovations to this end include radio, aviation and the internet. In more recent years Faith Comes by Hearing and other missions have been uploading Bible translations from all the world's languages to the internet in both written and audio form. Faith missionaries have not been oblivious to human suffering and social needs. Medical, agricultural and educational ministries have developed wherever they have gone. Faith missions today are some of the largest mission societies, working together in a spirit of cooperation all over the world. Together, they make the most powerful missionary force the world has ever known.

West Africa where I served for over fifty years used to be known as the white man's grave. Fortunately, vaccinations and anti-malarial drugs are now available which enable missionaries to survive. Despite inroads made by Islam from the north, fifty percent of the population of sub-Saharan Africa converted to Christianity in the twentieth century.

Bible translation can be viewed properly as a twentieth-century foreign-missions specialization, but it has its roots early in the history of the Christian church. By the 15th century there were more than thirty translations of the Bible, and in the next three centuries that number doubled. But what of the other seven-thousand languages that exist in the world, including at least seven-hundred in Papua New Guinea and five-hundred in Nigeria? The modern missionary movement changed the entire complexion of Bible translation. No longer was the work delegated to meticulous scholars in monasteries or musty libraries; it was being undertaken by untrained missionaries stationed all over the world who carried out their translation work in thatched-roof huts with illiterate language informants.

The Baptist missionary William Carey is regarded as the first and most prolific of missionary Bible Translators. In the 19th century Bible translations appeared in nearly five-hundred more languages. But in the twentieth century, with the introduction of the science of linguistics, translation work became a specialized ministry and missionary translators have felt compelled to provide the word of God in every language, a goal that is hoped to be fulfilled by 2025. Wycliffe Bible Translators, an organization started in 1934 by W. Cameron Townsend, has made an invaluable contribution to the progress of world evangelism. As "Cam" Townsend said: "The greatest missionary is the Bible in the mother tongue." Computers and specialized translation programs have speeded up the translation process and the associated task of dictionary making. Starting from scratch by learning a new language, deciphering its grammar and phonology and putting the language into writing, a Bible translation usually took over twenty years to complete. However, today, with better educated mother tongue speakers, translations are being done at a faster rate.

Jesus said, "And this gospel of the kingdom will be preached in the whole world as a testimony to all nations, and then the end will come" (Matthew 24:14).

PART 1

FINDING GOD'S WILL

CHILDHOOD EXPERIENCES

1940-1958

Ross and Stuart

My sister Libby (2017)

"What a beautiful skin Ross has," one of Mum's friends said. My Mum responded with: "It's only skin deep." She was no doubt referring to the fact that I was a naughty child with an impish face. They called me "Diz", an abbreviation of Disney, because the family thought I looked like one of Walt Disney's characters. I often had nightmares which would indicate some psychological stress. I would wake up screaming, much to the consternation of the family and especially the mothers of friends when I was sleeping over. A recurring dream had me sitting in a corner with the foreground streaming away from me.

We lived at Maffra in central Gippsland, Victoria, Australia. To the north and west were the mountains of the Great Dividing Range with snow on the higher peaks during winter. Thirty miles to the south was the sleepy beach village of Seaspray on the ninety-mile beach. Maffra was a dairy town with milk and butter factories. The climate was good, and I never wanted to move to a city.

My brother Stu was four years older than me and my sister Libby four years younger. My Dad's name was Prescott, usually addressed as Prec. He was a successful butcher. My father left school on his fourteenth birthday and started work in a grocer shop. His break came when he and his brother Bill put a bet on a racehorse. They had taken the horse, Froudwin, to Caulfield by train where they stayed the night. Next day they were going by train to Romsey, but the horse escaped and could not be loaded onto the train in the usual manner. It was finally caught and loaded onto the passenger train. At the racecourse the price lengthened to twenty to one, as the rumor got around that Froudwin had been on the loose all morning. Prescott and Bill won £400 when the horse won the race, and with this money they bought a butcher shop in Stratford.

Dad was a perfectionist, which paid off, because people do like quality meat. He bought his brother out when the latter married a farmer's daughter and then he bought another shop in Maffra, the small town where I was born in 1940. Dad started a pig farm and built abattoirs to slaughter his own meat. Later he bought a farm where he could fatten his animals to their prime. People came from far and wide to buy his sausages. He taught me to do a job well. I remember one occasion when he gave me his shoes to polish and I had to repeat the job a couple of times before he was satisfied. On another occasion he told me that there was only one perfect person who ever lived; Jesus Christ. He was brought up as a Presbyterian and loved singing in the church choir. He had singing lessons and used to sing opera in local concerts. I remember him singing around the piano with his rich tenor voice, together with buxom Auntie Ella. My parents had many friends who used to gather at each other's homes every month or so to eat and drink, play cards and have a good time.

My mother, Lorna, was known as Will. She was the daughter of the shire engineer at Stratford Shire. Her parents thought she was marrying below her class when she chose to marry the fledgling butcher, but Dad claimed later that he was the favorite son-in-law. Mum was a great sportswoman, winning trophies in tennis and golf and later in life in lawn bowls. I don't have such good memories of Mum. She was an alcoholic for the latter years of her life when I was at the sensitive age of ten-to-fifteen years old. It was hard coming home from primary school and finding Mum intoxicated in the bathroom with an empty bottle in her hand. It was even more embarrassing when I was with a friend. I fear that these experiences made me an insecure and immature teenager.

Mum was diagnosed with cancer after the birth of my sister and had a mastectomy at that time. Years later the cancer returned and who knows what pain she had to bear. I remember lying in bed at night and often hearing my parents arguing, I don't know what it was about, but it disturbed me. Dad liked his Scotch too much. I was a naughty child who threw stones on people's roofs and on one occasion broke into a milk factory and emptied a large box of empty condensed milk cans down a flight of stairs. The primary school principal called me into his office and asked if I was involved. Our gang didn't do it, I lied.

One summer Stu and I were coming home from Sunday school. We had a box of matches and in the vacant block opposite our house, we would light a match and throw it into the dry grass and then stamp out the fire. We did this a few times, until the fire got away from us. The fire brigade had to be called to put out the fire and Stu and I spent the rest of the day locked in our bedroom.

With Dad's financial success he bought a new Ford Customline every two years. We had nice family holidays at Lakes Entrance, Merimbula and even up to Sydney, and to visit cousins at Wyong. Oysters and crayfish were a treat at the seaside resorts. Having climbed the social ladder, Dad decided to send his children to prestigious Melbourne schools for the last four years of secondary school. The downside was that being four years apart from both brother and sister, we were separated from each other for most of our teenage years. We never got to know each other as well as children who are born closer together.

I was a boarder at Scotch College, Hawthorn, from 1955 to 1958. They were difficult years for me. I was immature, and my lack of sporting prowess made it difficult for me to be "one of the boys". I played football under duress and was reluctantly recruited into the army cadets. I joined the medical corps which was for slackers, not those who were looking for leadership training. I had no courage at all.

In the middle of my second year, at the age of fifteen, Mum died. I knew she was in hospital, but I wasn't told that she had cancer or was dying. I received a message that the house master wanted to see me at lunchtime. I couldn't think of any reason why he would want to see me, except that Mum had died. Sure enough, when I entered his office, in his gruff army fashion, he told me the news. My mouth sank at the edges and got stuck there, but I didn't burst into tears. I was to catch a train into Flinders Street Station the next morning where I would be met by an uncle I didn't know. I felt very much alone. I went to the church service but wasn't deemed mature enough to go to the burial. I missed out on having a mother's love during my teenage years, a hurdle I had to get over and only did so with God's help.

As a boarder in the 1950's all boys were expected to go to church on Sunday morning and to the school chapel service in the evening.

We also had general assembly each morning with a hymn, a Bible reading, and prayer. Neither this nor my previous attendance at Maffra Presbyterian Sunday School and church had given me a meaningful relationship with God. He was out there somewhere and although I had a respect for God and never blasphemed his name, he was rarely in my thoughts, and his word was not a conscious standard for my speech or behavior. Being a church school, Scotch believed in presenting the Christian moral standards to students, but not in trying to convert them. But without a true conversion experience, Christianity is just a nominal adherence to religion, without the spiritual power given by the Holy Spirit.

When the opportunity came to attend a confirmation class at the local Presbyterian church, I enthusiastically joined, but I was not introduced to Jesus in such a way that I found faith. So, nothing was confirmed and when I left school at the age of eighteen, I stopped going to church. I didn't leave my mark at this wonderful school; my only claim to fame was coming twelfth in the school cross-country race. This, even though I used to stop and have a smoke under a bridge during practice runs. In my final exams I managed to get second class honors in my two math subjects and win a Commonwealth scholarship which paid the fees for my pharmacy course.

LOST ADOLESCENCE

———◆◆◆———

1959-1962

"Therefore, if anyone is in Christ,
the new creation has come:
the old has gone, the new is here!"
2 Corinthians 5:17

Pharmacy was my career choice from the age of fourteen. I enjoyed Chemistry, Physics and Math at school, but shied away from languages and history and art subjects in general. I could do the first year of my four-year apprenticeship by correspondence, so I stayed home in Maffra living with Dad, Stu, my Dad's second wife, Flo, and two of her children.

On Christmas morning I accompanied Stu to a hotel in Newry where he wanted to have some Christmas drinks with friends. Not being into drinking yet, I asked if I could go for a drive while he was at the hotel. He agreed and told me not to do anything stupid. I was excited and took off along the country road a little bit too confidently. Coming to a bend in the road too fast, I slid in the gravel on the edge of the road and before I could straighten up, I hit a huge post, part of a bridge, which came loose, and the pick-up and I fell three meters down into the creek. I came to with the roar of the engine in my ears. I was under the steering wheel with my foot pressing on the accelerator. I turned off the motor and struggled out. I was standing in a few inches of water. I wasn't injured at all, but it was impossible to get the pick-up out of the creek without a tow-truck. Back on the road, I hitched a ride back to the hotel to break the news to Stu. I won't repeat what he called me. What a start to Christmas day! We were to spend Christmas with our cousins at my uncle and aunt's place. When we arrived, Stu explained that he had had an accident. Dad noticed the sheepish look on my face and said: "It was you that had the accident, wasn't it?"

After being in Melbourne for four years, I didn't have any friends in Maffra and I lived a very quiet life for the first nine months. Then I met Keith and Vince, two locals who liked a drink or two on the weekends and attendance at the local dance hall in Tinamba on Saturday nights. I loved being with them. I was accepted, and we enjoyed ourselves. I started smoking a packet of cigarettes a day and I also had an interest in the horses. Dad and my uncle were part owners of a racehorse and Dad was a member of the Flemington Race Club.

One weekend, the local Ford dealer loaned me a station wagon in the hope that I might buy it, or that Dad might buy it for me. I told my friends I had wheels for the weekend, where could we go? They said there was a party at Bairnsdale, about forty miles away. At two a.m. after too much drinking we set off home to Maffra. My friends soon fell asleep and then I followed suit. I woke up to find saplings flying past me right and left, and then a large tree loomed up ahead with a hump on one side of it. We hit the hump and the station wagon flipped over on its roof. We struggled out the windows, all uninjured except for some slight bleeding from broken glass. The station wagon was a write-off. We hitched a ride back to Maffra and I entered Dad's bedroom at four a.m. to announce that I had had another accident. I was quite sober by this stage, but not a popular boy. It was miraculous that none of us was hurt. I didn't realize it at the time, but I believe my heavenly Father was protecting me through my wayward youth.

In 1960 I went to Melbourne to live, so that I could attend Pharmacy College and continue my apprenticeship in Ashburton. I stayed with a Jewish couple on Dandenong Road, Windsor, friends of my step-mother Flo. The only noteworthy event that happened there was when Fred Wiesmayr, a migrant from Austria, came and shared my room for six months. He was keen on learning English well, and he used to lie on his bed in the evening reading through an English dictionary. He had entered training for the Catholic priesthood in Austria but became disenchanted when he saw a priest fossicking around in the garden picking up the wafers that had been prayed over and for Catholics had now become the body of Christ.

We had discussions on religion, but we were both ignorant of the ancient path where we could find rest for our souls. I took him to a Presbyterian church and he took me to a Catholic Church. We weren't impressed by either. Fred used to go and meditate in the St Kilda cemetery which was over the road from our flat. The truth was that we were both lost souls seeking the truth and not knowing where to find it.

A month after Fred left the flat, I heard that he had found God. He was now preaching on street corners. This was before the era of mobile phones, and I didn't know how I could contact him, but

I hoped that I would meet him again one day and find out what he had discovered.

I moved into a flat in Murrumbeena with a friend Jim Shanahan, a fellow Gippslander. We had a small circle of friends and our main activity was getting drunk on Saturday night and recovering from our hangovers on Sunday. We went to the footy, to horse races, car races and the occasional film. When I got my first car at the age of twenty-one, three of us drove to Darwin and back for a holiday, 2,500 miles each way. Between Port Augusta and Alice Springs, we put the car on the Ghan train which travelled through the desert very slowly.

One fateful weekend I went to Maffra to visit my family and spend time with my old friends Keith and Vince. We drank all afternoon at one of the Maffra hotels and left at six p.m., the time when the bars closed in that era. Keith was driving slowly up the main street and I pulled out to pass him. He accelerated, and I accelerated, and there we were racing up the main street. The police didn't catch us, but they did get my number. A couple of weeks later a policeman knocked on the door of our flat in Murrumbeena and asked if I was in Maffra on a certain day. I said it was likely, as that was my home town. The police "threw the book" at me. I was charged with numerous offences including dangerous driving, a criminal offence. I went to court in Maffra in fear and trembling and Dad procured a lawyer, but to no avail. I was found guilty on all counts, fined fifty pounds, and I lost my license for six months. Dad paid the fine and I left my car in Maffra. My life was going pear shaped. I had failed my final chemistry exam the year before and then I failed it for a second time six months later. Now I had lost my license and I was a convicted criminal for life.

In addition, I had a bad conscience. I felt that I was living a useless life, being of no help to anyone. My conscience was bothering me and at one stage I decided not to believe in God any more. That gave me relief, but it was very temporary. I found that I couldn't really believe that God didn't exist. I have always appreciated the beauty of creation, the stars in the sky, the mountains, the ocean, the animals and birds and insects. I believed in a Designer, but I couldn't see him. I hadn't yet found faith.

However, the "Hound of Heaven" was lurking in the background. I was a chosen vessel about to become a trophy of grace, a servant of the Almighty God.

Born Again

August 12th, 1963

Fred and Janet Wiesmayr (2016)

August 12ᵗʰ 1963 was the most significant day of my life. I was nearly twenty-three and my life was about to change dramatically. The One who had protected me through several car accidents had been drawing me to himself through disappointments and a feeling of inadequacy. Jesus said: "No one can come to me unless the Father who sent me draws them" (John 6:44). This is how God did it for me.

Having lost my license, I had to go to work by train. I was walking to the Murrumbeena station in the morning with cigarette in hand when my Austrian acquaintance Fred saw me, the one who had found God and preached on street corners. I hadn't seen him for two years. He tapped me on the shoulder and called my name. I acknowledged him, and he invited me to come to his house the following Monday night. As 'fate' would have it, he was living in the street behind me. I said to myself: "I must ask him what happened a couple of years back", but as soon as I got in the door, he had a Bible in my hand and was explaining the gospel to me. He said he could see I wasn't a real Christian. I needed to repent and believe that Jesus had died on the cross for my sins. In short, I had to surrender my life to the Lord Jesus Christ. It took a bit of convincing that I wasn't a Christian; that statement was a shock to me. But I knew in my heart that I wasn't living God's way. I didn't want to give up my independence; I wasn't going to give it up without a fight. My last line of defense was evolution. If evolution is true as most of the scientists believe, then maybe I didn't have to believe in God, and I could stay as I was. At midnight Fred's wife, Janet, wanted to go to bed in the lounge-room, as the bedroom was being painted, so Fred said: "Ross, do you want to become a Christian or not?" I succumbed and said yes. We knelt down, and Fred asked me to pray and confess my sins and ask Jesus into my life. I was a shy person and I couldn't get any words out. I asked Fred to pray for me, which he did. He said goodnight feeling that he hadn't really got through to me, but I had made a sincere decision.

When I arrived home, I threw my pack of cigarettes up on a cupboard in my bedroom and made a vow that I would never smoke again. If I was going to be a Christian, I wanted to be a real one this time. I would repent of my sin and turn my back on what I knew to be wrong in my life. Fred didn't tell me what I should do, I decided it myself. I vowed that I wouldn't smoke again, I wouldn't drink beer again, and I wouldn't bet on the horses any more. I had no trouble giving up the cigarettes; I never smoked another one in my life. Giving them up was easy, I had a motivation which inspired me. I wanted to be healthy for God and obedient to him.

Two days later Stu called in to my apartment with a couple of bottles of beer in tow. He poured me a glass without asking me, and I was too scared to say anything. I took a small sip, and that was the last time I tasted beer. Some members of my family had an alcohol problem, and I was convinced that I would be better off without it. I never had a bet on the horses again either, but it took a while to wean myself off the form guide. I had a system and I loved to see if I could pick the winners.

My mates soon noticed the change in me, and our relationship became strained. How could we get along together, now that I didn't drink or smoke or talk about the horses any longer. Moreover, I had started to go to church and spend time with new friends.

Stu heard about the change in my life and went home and told Dad that I had been caught up in some cult. One Sunday morning not long after, I came home from church to find Dad's car parked outside our flat. That hadn't happened before; I was perplexed. I went inside and had an emotional altercation with Dad and Flo. I tried to convince them that I wasn't caught up in a cult; I was attending the local Baptist church which was orthodox in belief. Dad said: "But we are all Christians. Why do you have to go overboard and stop doing this, that and the other? You are going too far!" I told him that I wanted to be a real Christian and turn from anything I thought was wrong or unhelpful.

After a month I moved out of Jim's flat and moved in with Fred and family. I started to get a feel of what biblical Christianity was like and I was amazed when I tried to think of 'real' Christians I had known in the past. There was nobody. There was not one relative that fell into that category, and not one friend, present or past. When a Christian girl from Maffra, named Nancy, heard about my conversion, she said: "He is the last person in Maffra I expected to find the Lord." I couldn't think of anyone who might have been praying for me, but later I learned that Nancy's mother had put my name in her little black book and started praying for me after I attended one of her Christian meetings at high school eight years previously.

A friend named Len Pearce lived in a nearby town. The last time we met was in a pub at Lakes Entrance. He was converted six months before me and after my conversion, when he told his mates at the Stratford Football Club that Ross Jones had also been born again, the answer came, "If Ross Jones has become a Christian, then it's possible for anyone!" Len became a missionary and served God for many years with the Red Sea Mission Team in the Middle East.

What happened to me on the twelfth of August 1963? There are many biblical expressions to describe my experience. I was converted, born again, justified, put right with God, and made a child of God. I was forgiven all my sins, I was saved, I received the gift of eternal life, I received the gift of the Holy Spirit, and many more blessings as well. I would like to explain some of these.

I once asked a Nigerian whether he was born again. "No," he said, "I still watch television." Another Nigerian told me some girls weren't born again, because they wore high-heel shoes. Obviously, people get the experience of being born again confused with their brand of holiness. Being born again, according to John's Gospel chapter three, is an internal change that takes place when a person is born of the Spirit of God. It is a transformation that occurs when God's Spirit enters the life of a believer and transforms his attitudes and behavior. The Spirit gives a new quality of life called "eternal life". The former things pass away, all becomes new. When the Spirit of God came on the disciples in the book of Acts, they were described as having been filled with boldness, joy and peace. That was happening to me too.

When I woke up the morning after giving my life to Christ, I had a sense of excitement, because I knew I had done something significant and believed that God would be faithful. I started to read

Matthew's Gospel and was a bit disappointed that it was the same as I had read before. But several weeks later my heart was suddenly filled with joy, and I realized that I was a child of God, saved for eternity, and saved for a purpose: to be a witness for Christ. The boldness didn't come immediately; it built up gradually over the next twelve months. I sat down and wrote letters to all my friends and relatives, telling them that I had decided to follow Jesus and live the life of faith. No one responded, except some who wished me well. I talked to people at work about the Lord and invited them to special meetings at Murrumbeena Baptist church. I got involved in the youth group and in teaching a Sunday school class.

The Bible is God's message to mankind. It is a complex book, itself made up of sixty-six books written by many authors, most of whom were Jewish. It was written in Hebrew and Greek and the precious truths found within it are couched in Middle Eastern culture. It is a mixture of history, prophecies, praise songs, letters and apocalyptic prophecies. Who can hope to understand the Bible overnight? The Holy Spirit opened my eyes and gave me spiritual discernment, but it still took years of Bible study, listening to sermons and the like, before I felt that I had a good grasp on the many facets of Christian theology.

Another aspect of my salvation was that I was what the Bible calls "justified" or "put right with God". Romans 5:1 says: "Therefore, since we have been justified through faith, we have peace with God through our Lord Jesus Christ." Justification is a legal term. It is as if we have been judged already and given the verdict "not guilty". When translating this verse into Boko in later years, it came out literally like this: "As God has acquitted us because of the faith we express, we are now on good terms with him, through the power of our Lord Jesus Christ." It was a wonderful revelation for me to realize that I was acquitted; my sins were all forgiven, buried in the deepest sea. "As far as the east is from the west, so far has he removed our transgressions from us" (Psalm 103:12). Another passage that impressed me greatly was Ephesians 2:8-9, "For it is by grace you have been saved, through faith - and this is not from yourselves, it is the gift of God – not by works, so that no one can boast. For we are God's handiwork, created in Christ Jesus to do good works, which God prepared in advance for us to do."

One day I was travelling in the country with evangelists from Open Air Campaigners (OAC). We had a meal at the house of some Christians who had invited us, and they had a guest booklet near the front door where guests could write their name and address and some nice comment, especially a spiritual word of wisdom. I thought for a long time for an impressive comment and ended up simply writing: "Saved by grace". Evangelist Bryan Greenwood said to me later: "Your pastor would be very proud of you for making that statement." Amazing grace! Grace is a word that easily rolls off the tongue, but it is impossible to plumb the depths of God's grace, that undeserved kindness whereby my sins are forgiven and I am accepted; not because I go to church regularly, or read the Bible, or do great exploits, or fast and pray, or lead a respectable life, but simply because I put my faith in the Lord Jesus Christ.

What did that mean? It meant that I believed in Jesus, I believed in the incarnation, that God himself was born as a human baby at Bethlehem. I believed that he lived a perfect life and that he died on the cross in my place, taking the penalty for my sins. I believed that Jesus is God, God the Son, the second person of the holy Trinity. "In the beginning was the Word, and the Word was with God, and the Word was God" (John 1:1).

EARLY SPIRITUAL GROWTH

1963-1965

With "Archie" and aboriginal children

Conversion for me was a coming to know God. Before he was some force out there in the blue, now he was God whom I learnt to know personally, who lived with me and promised never to leave or forsake me. It took some time and I struggled to grow over the coming months, but grow I did, and this is how it happened.

Fully committed and busy learning, on Tuesday nights I was at the OAC prayer and Bible study group, Wednesday night I was at the Murrumbeena Baptist church mid-week Bible study, Thursday night I was at a Melbourne Bible Institute lecture with my pastor Max Kingdom, Friday night I was getting practical experience at Norman's Corner with OAC, Saturday night I was with the Murrumbeena youth group, and on Sunday night I was at the evening church service.

Church at Murrumbeena during the 1960's was a truly exhilarating experience. The pastor and his wife were humble people, but his preaching was powerful. I remember one night when as an illustration he spoke about the famous Italian violinist Niccolo Paganini. During a concert a string on his violin broke. Undaunted he kept playing until another string broke and then another. Then he calmly announced: "One string and Paganini". The pastor was illustrating the biblical truth that with Christ all things are possible for us to do. Such teaching inspired me.

The singing at Murrumbeena was spine-tingling. I had been brought up in a staid Presbyterian church where the organist was too slow and some of the hymns too old. In comparison the pianist at Murrumbeena, Bill Bertram hammered away at the keys with great gusto and it seemed as if everyone in the building was giving it their best. I was soaking in God's word at every opportunity and the words of Charles Wesley's famous hymns would put me in an ecstatic state as we praised the Lord. As an example, let me quote one of his hymns. Just read the words and absorb the theological truths contained within. Understand it all and you understand the gospel.

And can it be that I should gain
an interest in the Savior's blood?
Died He for me, who caused His pain,
for me, who Him to death pursued?
Amazing love! How can it be
that Thou, my God, shouldest die for me?
Tis mystery all, the Immortal dies.
Who can explore His strange design?
In vain the firstborn seraph tries
to sound the depths of love divine.
Tis mercy all! Let earth adore,
let angel minds inquire no more.
He left His Father's throne above,
so free, so infinite His grace.
Emptied Himself of all but love
and bled for Adam's helpless race.
Tis mercy all, immense and free,
for O my God, it found out me!
Long my imprisoned spirit lay,
fast bound in sin and nature's night.
Thine eye diffused a quickening ray,
I woke, the dungeon flamed with light.
My chains fell off, my heart was free,
I rose, went forth, and followed Thee.

No condemnation now I dread,
Jesus, and all in Him, is mine.
Alive in Him, my living Head,
and clothed in righteousness divine.
Bold I approach the eternal throne
and claim the crown, through Christ my own.
Charles Wesley (1707-1788)

A couple of months after my conversion I decided to prepare
for baptism. I had been christened as a child, but I saw no examples

or support in the New Testament to authenticate this practice. What I saw was "repent and be baptized" and "as many as believed were baptized". So, I became convinced that baptism was for adult believers and that baptism should be by immersion of the whole body in water, not by sprinkling. The Greek word for "baptize" means to dip or immerse. In December I was baptized by immersion and simultaneously became a member of Murrumbeena Baptist Church where I remained a member for thirty years.

This church had a strong emphasis on overseas mission work and during the 1960's they prayerfully and financially supported sixteen members in foreign mission work.

When I began my Christian life, I had a debt at the pharmacy where I worked. I saw my first financial responsibility as paying off that debt, about fifty pounds. Once that was done, I thought about my financial responsibility towards God, about being generous, about tithing and freewill offerings. I saved up another fifty ponds and gave it to Bryan for the evangelistic work of OAC. I felt that they were on the front lines of the spiritual battle, doing what Christ had commanded: "You are the light of the world. ... Let your light shine before others" (Matthew 5:14, 16).

After giving that first gift I had a sinking feeling that I had wasted my hard-earned money. I could have used it for my own needs or pleasure. The answer was clear: "If God is there, then I did the right thing, and he will bless me." I never again had a problem with giving; it was an accepted responsibility that I would give at least ten percent of my income to the Lord; to my church, to evangelistic ministry and foreign missionary work, or to help the poor.

What helped my spiritual development most was practical experience with OAC. When Fred left the flat in Windsor, he met a Christian girl, Janet, whom he started going out with. She took him to an evangelistic meeting at the Melbourne Bible Institute in Armadale. The evangelist that night was Bryan Greenwood, the Victorian director of OAC. After the meeting Fred approached him and said, "What right do you have to oppose the pope?" He was clinging to his last line of defense as I had with my questions on evolution. But that night Fred gave his life to Christ. After that Fred became a voluntary worker with OAC, accompanying and helping the evangelists in their ministry. So, when I became a disciple of Jesus, Fred took me along and introduced me to the OAC evangelists. There was a Bible study and prayer time every Tuesday night at Flinders Lane in the city, and an open-air meeting on the corner of Collins and Russell streets, also known as Norman's corner, on Friday nights. The atmosphere was very challenging and different, but I became a voluntary worker too, and a regular attender at these meetings. For several months I wanted to join in the extemporaneous prayer time at the prayer meetings, but my nervousness hindered me. Once I made the plunge and got some words out, it became easy.

Norman's Corner was more challenging. I was terrified that I would be asked to do something and sometimes suffered diarrhea as a result of my timidity. But the Holy Spirit gradually did his work in transforming me to be a bold person. The evangelists were extroverts, with musical, artistic and rhetorical skills. One evening one of them danced around a hat that had been put on the footpath crying out: "It's alive! It's alive!" When a sufficient crowd had gathered, he lifted the hat to reveal a Bible, and then he went on to explain that the Bible was the living Word of God that contained good news: Christ had died on the cross for our sins, so that we might be forgiven and reconciled to God!

Eventually I was asked to get up on the box and share the meaning of a relevant Bible verse. After that trial, I progressed to giving my testimony and later learnt how to do some sketches in meetings while the evangelist was preaching. I used special chalk which glowed when an ultra-violet light was turned on and the crowd would hum with amazement. Drunks like to get involved in open air discussions, and they could either ruin a presentation, or the evangelist could turn the altercation to his advantage and get his message across, while the crowd stood watching the spectacle. OAC taught me to have a concern for the "lost", those myriads of people who don't know God, who have no sense of purpose in their lives, and who get enslaved by all sorts of bad habits. Jesus called them sheep without a shepherd. I was so glad that the Good Shepherd had found me and was guiding me step by step to full-time Christian service. Bryan became a mentor for me for a couple of years and fifty-five years later we are still good friends.

Working as a voluntary worker with OAC was wonderful training for future service for the Lord. Bryan and many others contributed to my spiritual growth. My pastor Max Kingdom has been mentioned. Rev. Neville Horn was a member of my church and I attended monthly missionary meetings at his home. This brought me into contact with missionaries and their work. He also had a daughter, Joy, with whom I was spending more and more time.

I struggled through much of this time to have a regular "Quiet Time". My ideal was to spend an hour with God at six a.m. every morning, but it was a struggle. I also wanted to win many people to Christ, but that wasn't happening either, despite lots of activity and prayer on my part. My pastor said that not everyone is born to be a soul winner. Nevertheless, I was determined to serve God and as I thought about it, there seemed to be two choices: become a pastor or a missionary. Because of my adventurous spirit and perhaps lack of compassion to be dealing daily with people's problems, I told the Lord that I wanted to serve him on the mission field. I just didn't know what country I should go to, or what work I should do there. I was not keen on being a missionary pharmacist, as my experience with Open Air Campaigners had taught me the importance of evangelism.

Verses like Matthew 6:33 took control of my mind: "But seek first his kingdom and his righteousness, and all these things will be given to you as well." Maybe I could leave pharmacy and spend my life serving God. Another command of Jesus, his final words in Matthew's Gospel, seemed to me to be the big job that he wanted the Church to concentrate on. After his resurrection he gathered his disciples together and he said to them majestically: "All authority in heaven and on earth has been given to me. Therefore go and make disciples of all nations, baptizing them in the name of the Father and of the Son and of the Holy Spirit, and teaching them to obey everything I have commanded you. And surely, I am with you always, to the very end of the age" (Matthew 28:18-20). Yes! That command wasn't just for the apostles, it was also for me! And it is accompanied by a promise. He would be with me to guide and strengthen and protect me wherever I went.

From memory I thought I sold my car to pay for my Bible School fees, but on reading a journal I kept at the time, I found I sold it for another reason. I had read a couple of books about Hudson Taylor, an early missionary to China. Back in the nineteenth century missionaries often lived in great poverty and after reading about it I decided I had better practice poverty myself. I was living with a Mrs Reid at the time in Murrumbeena. She was a farmer's widow and a good cook, and she used to look after me like a son, with eggs and bacon and fried banana for breakfast! I felt that this was too luxurious and that I should move out, but later decided to stay until Christmas when I would go off to work with OAC during January. I also felt at the time that owning a car was too luxurious. I could give the five pounds that it cost to run it each week to the Lord! I even contemplated selling my radio and electric razor so that I would only be left with my clothes and books.

Within two years of my conversion I had decided to go to Bible School. Melbourne Bible Institute wasn't far away and had a good reputation. I asked Bryan, my pastor Max Kingdom, and the Rev Neville Horn, to write references for me. I went to Maffra to tell my parents. As expected, Dad wasn't enthusiastic about it, but he said he was in favor of it, if that was what I wanted. He didn't want to lose me, as he thought he would, but said that I would be doing others a lot of good.

The Call to Dahomey

July 2nd, 1966

Animal skulls in Cotonou market for use in black magic

I found life at the Melbourne Bible Institute (MBI), Armadale, to be really enjoyable. The principal, the Rev Dr Graeme Miller, suggested that I do a Licentiate of Theology. My pharmacy qualification was only a diploma, because at that time the Pharmacy College was not affiliated with a university, so I could not do a Bachelor of Divinity or Theology which were post-graduate degrees. He also suggested that I study Greek and Hebrew and master the first-year Greek course before Easter!

I was happy, but I was concerned about Dad who had told me that his last years were going to be his saddest. He suffered from arthritis in the knees and his second marriage to Flo was not all that successful. Over the years I often tried to talk to him about Jesus, but after a few minutes he would say: "That's enough". I could only pray for him. During the holidays I travelled home by train to visit him and on that occasion, he turned the TV off and asked me about the devil and hell.

On Sunday I had my first opportunity to preach in a church, at Stratford Presbyterian church. Dad and Flo came to hear me together with brother Stu and sister Libby and some other relatives. I was so excited to have this opportunity to preach to them from the pulpit. They thought I did a good job, and Dad and Libby said they were proud of me.

Greek and Hebrew took up most of my study time; I could get good marks with the other subjects without much study. I was continually reading devotional books in my spare time. Each week we had a missionary speaker from various parts of the world. I found their presentations very interesting as I continued to wait on the Lord to show me where I should go and what I should do. But how would I know? How would God show me?

On July 2nd 1966 I attended a Sudan Interior Mission (SIM) youth meeting in Kew, where missionary Shirley Barby was speaking about her work in Dahomey. Another missionary, Gordon Helyer, spoke about his work in Somalia. I had an attraction towards Africa and was very much interested in what Shirley was saying. There were unreached tribes in the jungles and savannah of inland Dahomey and a need for Bible translation work. After the talks, the sixty or so youth present broke up into three groups to pray. I hoped I would be chosen for the West African group, and sure enough I was. I prayed and said I was ready to go. A girl said: "You prayed as if you really meant it tonight." I replied: "I think the Lord has spoken to me tonight."

I shared a room with six other men at MBI, and when I entered the room that night, I said: "I think the Lord has called me to Dahomey." They said: "Where?" I said "Dahomey!" They said: "We've never heard of it. Go to sleep. When you wake up in the morning you will have forgotten all about it." But, no! When I woke up, I awoke with excitement in my heart, believing that God had indeed called me to serve him in Dahomey. I could do nothing over the next two days but look up information on West Africa in the encyclopedia and in mission booklets. The climate was harsh, disease prevalent. In fact, it was called the white man's grave. But that didn't daunt me. I had spoken to Shirley after the meeting and she had given me the name and address of a Canadian missionary and suggested I write to him.

I wrote to Roland Pickering and prayed that God would confirm his call through Roland's response. It took more than three weeks for the letter to reach him, so I had to wait some time for his reply. My study was sacrificed, because all I could think about was Dahomey. Shirley came and spoke again at MBI, and the same appeal and desire was aroused in me.

The following Saturday night was a missionary rally at MBI and there was to be a film. I prayed: "Lord, if this film is about Dahomey, I'll go there, taking it as a confirmation that you have called me." The film was called: "This child shall be a slave". It began in Upper Volta, moved to Niger Republic and the second half of the film was all in Dahomey! Coincidence? Nobody could convince me of that. The Scripture Union notes I had started reading on July 1st had a passage from Isaiah six for July 2nd in which the question was asked: "Whom shall I send? And who will go for us?" And I said: "Here am I. Send me!" (Isaiah 6:8).

The reply from Roland arrived. The stamp which was mainly black pictured an African tapestry and looked beautiful to my eyes. Roland was very positive and finished his letter by saying: "Your call to Dahomey is most likely a true one, so do not let anything keep you from getting here." He said he was interested to hear that I was studying Greek and Hebrew and told me to keep at it. I saw the Lord's hand in that, because it wasn't my idea to study Hebrew before I arrived at MBI, and it was the first year that Hebrew was taught there. He also suggested that I think about doing a linguistics course with Wycliffe Bible translators. Wow! I was on my way.

This 'call' has been a great strength in my life and Christian service. When the disciples saw the risen Christ, they were transformed from being weak followers of Jesus to being bold witnesses. They went out with confidence and spread the good news of Jesus Christ to all the surrounding countries. My confidence in God was similar. He had shown me what country he wanted me to work in, and the kind of work he wanted me to do. This gave me great enthusiasm and commitment to serve him with SIM - for my whole life if necessary.

I just had one niggling doubt. At school I hated languages, even English. My interest was in mathematics and the sciences. Why would God call me into Bible translation?

In September I was part of an evangelistic team that went to King Island in Bass Strait with OAC for a major campaign. One of my responsibilities was cooking for the team. We were excited when thirty children wrote notes expressing their desire to ask Jesus into their hearts, and thirty teenagers responded positively. On the final night ten adults made decisions to surrender to Christ. One member of the team was David Cummings, who later became Australian director of Wycliffe Bible Translators. I told him about being perplexed that God would call me to do Bible translation when I didn't have a love for languages. He immediately asked me what I was like at math. "Oh, that's my favorite subject," I said. "Well that is what you need for language analysis and translation" he said. If you are good at math, you have an analytical mind and will make a good linguist. Hmm! The Lord didn't allow me to do two math subjects in my Matriculation year for nothing, even though it was five years before I found him.

I went and saw Rev. Miller, the MBI principal, about my call and renewed plans. He was thrilled that the Lord had guided me in such a clear way and approved of my plan of finishing my theology diploma at MBI, doing a linguistics course with the Summer Institute of Linguistics (SIL), and leaving for Dahomey in mid-1968.

In October I spent an hour with my pastor and told him about these recent events in my life. He said the guidance was clear and that Murrumbeena Baptist Church would stand behind me. Then I shared my experiences with Rev. Neville Horn. He was keen for me not to abandon my idea of doing a Bachelor of Divinity. But I only had one thing on my mind now, and that was getting to Dahomey as soon as possible. I eventually abandoned the idea of doing a B.D. Next was a visit to Mr. Quinton, the SIM State secretary. He gave me application papers to become a missionary with SIM. I was happy that my interviews with all these respected men had gone smoothly. They all felt that the guidance I had received from God was clear and genuine.

I met with the SIM council in April 1967 and they expressed favor in accepting me, but suggested I continue with my studies and reapply when my studies were finishing. Later, they said they would leave it to my conviction as to whether I went on with BD studies. I was officially accepted into SIM in November.

I had many discussions with my friend Joy Horn at this time. She also felt called to serve God as a missionary in West Africa, so we had plans to serve God together there. But I was in a hurry to get to Dahomey and I knew that if she was to be accepted as a long-term missionary with SIM, she would first have to attend Bible school for two years as well as fulfil a teaching bond for another two years. So, we decided that I should go to Dahomey for an initial four-year term and then, God willing, we would get married and go to Dahomey together.

In August we decided to say goodbye without any definite future commitment to each other. We went to church together and agreed that our friendship had been beneficial all around.

In my first year at MBI, Rev. John Smith was the leader of evangelistic activities and I was his offsider. In the second year I was a senior student which taught me valuable lessons in responsibility and gave me more confidence as a leader. During much of my devotional time while at MBI I was preoccupied with the desire for holiness. I wanted to be pure and holy for my Lord and a man of prayer, but I always seemed to fall short of the ideal. I have since learnt to be at peace with myself, accepting my limitations, while never ceasing to want to grow and mature.

GOD'S PROVISION

---◆---

1967-1969

Joy Horn, Bachelor of Arts

In September we had an OAC campaign in the Maffra-Heyfield area. It was encouraging to see several siblings and cousins of people with whom I went to school making decisions for Christ.

Four of the OAC team came to my parents' home for dinner one night and another four came the next night. On the second occasion, Jim Vine took the electronic organ inside and played hymns. After dinner we showed Dad some slides of the work. At the end Bryan said to Dad: "The greatest thing Ross would like to see before leaving for Africa would be for you to become a Christian." Dad responded that he had seen a complete change in me. He said, we lived in a different world and we were very happy people. Then he added: "We hope that we are all Christians, but you are a different kind to us, and the work you are doing is wonderful. You had better go before you get me."

Dad, Flo and brother Stu came down to Melbourne for my graduation from Bible school. Several days later I was with them in Maffra. I decided to spend a day in prayer to pray specifically for my financial needs. I needed several thousand dollars for my trip to Europe the following year, and I also needed forty people who would commit themselves to pray for me and support me financially with one dollar a week. SIM called it the "Forty Fellowship". But my most pressing need was $300 to get me up to Brisbane and to pay for the ten-week SIL linguistics course I would do there.

I found a quiet spot a few miles from home and sat in the car praying. I was claiming some promises from the Bible. Jesus said: "And I will do whatever you ask in my name" (John 14:13), and more specifically, "And my God will meet all your needs according to the riches of his glory in Christ Jesus" (Philippians 4:19). Dad scoffed at the idea that the Lord provides all our need and said he had to work hard for all he got! Next day there was nothing in the mail for me, but after dinner Flo had a talk with me and said she was concerned about my finances. She very sacrificially gave me $40 and said she would have to book things up until after Christmas. Then Dad asked me my position and gave me $200. I wasn't expecting my prayer to be answered in this way. Then Stuart gave me $10 for Christmas. Joy had got in early and given me $20, so I now had $270.

Next day at Spencer Street station Bryan was seeing me off, and he said to me that I would be tired sitting up for the one-thousand-mile trip from Melbourne to Brisbane. I had an intensive course to do. So, he paid $30 to change my ticket to a sleeper. The $300 I requested was complete. When working for a faith mission, there is no guaranteed salary. Missionaries have to trust in the Lord for their financial needs which come mainly through their personal support team. The Lord who provides has looked after me in this way all my life.

I loved the linguistics course more than any study I had ever done before, especially phonemics and grammar. My analytical mind reveled in it, and I got good marks.

Back in Melbourne again I had several months to get a support team together. I needed a Forty Fellowship team, prayer supporters, and enough money to pay for my fare to Africa, an advanced linguistics course in England, and nine-month's French study in Albertville, France.

Beginning in September friends had been telling me they would be praying or supporting me in my missionary work. There were so many gifts during March and April, anything from $1 - $500, but most of them were ten dollars or less. How different to 2019 when similar gifts are in the hundreds or even thousands of dollars! Friends Phil & Vivienne Edwards gave me three months free board, another lady gave me a camera, and Dad fixed my brakes. I spoke at many churches and home meetings and Bryan took me on a trip through country Victoria where I spoke to OAC supporters. Ninety percent of my Forty Fellowship had been promised by June. I had several hundred prayer supporters, a printer, Bob Coyle of Classic Press, who said he would print my quarterly prayer letters for as long as I needed, and a friend, Isabel, who said she would post them out for me each time.

My commissioning service at Murrumbeena Baptist church with the laying on of hands by the elders was held on June 30th. Over three-hundred friends and well-wishers packed the church. I flew out of Australia from Essendon airport with one suitcase on July 1st, 1968, farewelled by my parents, Joy, and several MBI students holding up a placard with the words, "Christ for Dahomey". I wasn't apprehensive, or sad at leaving everyone behind. I was excited about what lay ahead in Thailand, Israel, UK, France and eventually, Dahomey.

At no extra cost I could stop over at Bangkok and Jerusalem for a couple of days on the way to London. In Thailand I learnt I had to be careful not to get 'ripped off' by those who prey on tourists. At Jerusalem I decided to explore the holy city by myself. I had a great time climbing the city wall and walking around some of the perimeter. I took a bus to Bethlehem and Jericho, climbed the Mount of Olives, walked around the temple area and visited the garden tomb. Even though it was the year after the 'seven-day war', security was less strict then than it is today. It was helpful to see with my own eyes the places I had read about in the Bible and that I would be translating about in the future.

At London I proceeded to the SIL linguistics school at an old army camp in Surrey. It was out of the metropolitan area, in lovely English countryside with its narrow lanes and many trees and hedges. On the first day, a list of twenty-five books and articles was given to us to summarize, about three a week. I was in a dormitory with nine other men, and we had practical chores to do for an hour each day, especially in the kitchen. We had daily lectures in phonetics, phonology and grammar and half an hour a day with a language informant. My informant was Habton who spoke Tigrinya, a language of northern Ethiopia. It was so hard to mimic the guttural throat sounds he made, similar to Arabic.

In September I took a channel steamer to Boulogne, in France, and from there I took a train to Paris, and another train from there to Albertville in the beautiful French Alps. The French school in Albertville was only for missionaries. Twenty of us were bathed in a French atmosphere. Speaking English was forbidden. I fondly remember walking through the snow early in the morning to buy a bag of baguettes (French bread sticks). There were four hours of French lectures every day, but we had to concentrate on listening to and speaking French all day. I had studied French at school for five years, but I didn't remember much because it wasn't my thing.

Out of the front and back windows of our flat were 1,500 - 2,000-meter mountains which were not far away. The scenery was magnificent. Max, another Aussie, and I hired motor scooters one day and drove ninety miles through the mountains to Lausanne in Switzerland. On the way back, we had to insulate ourselves from the cold with newspaper stuck under our shirts. On another occasion all the students went by bus to Mount Blanc which was only thirty miles away and 15,781 ft high. We also went skiing on many occasions in winter.

We took part in many evangelistic activities while at Albertville. The most memorable for me was when I was distributing invitations to some houses. While knocking on a door, a big Alsatian came and stared at me. I froze and started walking stiffly out the drive. It came and snapped at my leg, making a hole in my trousers, but not injuring me.

I had ideas of spending the Christmas holidays in Spain or at a youth camp in Switzerland, but the Lord told me to stay home. I planned to pray for my posting in Dahomey and my forthcoming ministry. I received notice the day the holidays began that I would be working among the Boko people at a place called Segbana, so I prayed for them and spent four days in prayer without food or drink. An American couple, Bob and Carol-Lee Blaschke were working there, but they did not have training in linguistics, so my job would be to teach literacy and give the Boko people the Scriptures in their own language. I have always felt that this time of prayer laid a solid foundation for the work that I would be involved in for many years.

In February I received news that over $3,000 had been given for my travel and studies and that my Forty Fellowship team was complete. Nevertheless, when I was leaving France, I had to borrow $50 from my Australian friend.

I sailed from Marseilles on June 20th on the 'Jean Mermoz' and was accompanied by Swiss missionaries Franz and Margrit Kropf, who were also travelling to Dahomey to serve God with SIM. We stopped briefly at the ports of Casablanca in Morocco, Dakar in Senegal, Abidjan in Ivory Coast, Pointe Noire in Congo, Libreville in

Gabon, Douala in Cameroon and Lagos in Nigeria, before arriving in Dahomey on July 9th, 1969.

On the boat I had some good discussions with some Congolese men about polygamy. Should polygamous believers be baptized or not? These talks confirmed my opinion that new believers should not be expected to chase one wife and her children away, and that as believers they had the right to be baptized. Up to this time, that had been anathema to SIM leadership.

I wasn't going to Dahomey for humanitarian reasons, to lift a backward people into a Western style of life, or to tell the Boko people that they are children of God ignorant of their salvation. No, I was there to give them the Word of God in their own language, so that through faith in the Lord Jesus Christ they might find salvation from the power of sin and the gift of eternal life. I arrived in Dahomey with confidence, because it was God who had shown me that Bible translation was to be my chief task. Segbana and the Boko people were not my idea ether, it was God who guided the SIM council to send me there. My sufficiency would be from God who qualified me to be a missionary through the indwelling presence of the Holy Spirit.

PART 2

PLANTING THE BOKO CHURCH

Getting Started

1969-1971

My friend Bandanki at his farm

I have never been your average missionary. I was more like one of those despised fellows who had 'gone native'. One of the first things I noticed after arriving in Dahomey was that the mission stations were well out of town. That surprised me and disappointed me. I wanted to have a close relationship with the local people. I wanted, as much as possible, to eat Boko food, dress like them, have them as my friends, and treat them as equals. During my years in Africa I never had a need to be with my fellow missionaries, which was a bit difficult in Dahomey, as the missionary force of about sixty came from so many different countries, most of them francophone, and there were only a few Australians. I did enjoy spending time with my fellow missionaries, but it wasn't a need I had, until I got married. My wife very much needed to see another white face at least every two months.

At Segbana, the mission station was right next to the African houses, and my house was a large round hut consisting of mud walls and a grass roof cleverly woven and tied to a swamp-palm frame. I loved that hut which my American co-workers, Bob and Carol-Lee Blaschke had kindly prepared for me. It was whitewashed and had a cement floor and was divided in two by a wall. Half the hut was for my living quarters and half for my office. It even had a flush toilet! A group of Boko Christians lived in the adjoining quarter of Segbana. One of them, Isifu, became my helper, doing domestic chores and teaching me Boko language and culture. The Boko people were clean, well-built, subsistence farmers, working most days in their maize and cotton fields. Common sounds in town were the beating of drums and the rhythmic sounds of the women pounding grain in the large wooden mortars. They had few possessions apart from their clothes. Some owned a horse or a bicycle, others a radio or torch or kerosene lantern. They lived in compounds which consisted of half a dozen huts grouped in a circle or square with a common kitchen in the middle where the women prepared pap from crushed grain and an accompanying soup. Dogs, sheep, goats, chickens, and the occasional pig roamed freely.

Bob Blaschke had been teaching literacy at a village called Bobena, seventeen miles away, so we went there for a week to teach literacy to twenty young men. At the end of the week they all expressed their desire to continue in the Jesus way. Although I had just arrived, I could teach them also. I knew whether they were reading the Boko words correctly or not. No one there knew English, and only a few had a smattering of French. The leader of the young men was called Bandanki, which means chief of the bird-watchers, that is, the children who watch out for parrots which would come and eat the maturing corn.

I started going to Bobena for three days each week, living in Bandanki's compound. Many people would come to greet me and give me food. The people were keen to learn about Jesus, but it wasn't easy for them to break with their old way of life, which included polygamy, fetish worship, beer drinking and dance society connections with its associated immorality.

Isifu and I went to another village called Saonzi in September. While Isifu was teaching fifty children some Christian songs in Boko, fifty adults gathered around. Isifu then taught them about Jesus. This was typical of the great opportunities there were for preaching the gospel to a semi-Islamized animistic society.

On a later visit to Saonzi, two young men were among those who heard the message. Soon after, they went hunting and one said to the other: "We have seen the white man come to our village and tell us about Jesus, but we are already learning about Islam. Which way is right? Is it Islam that the majority is following? Or is it the Jesus way?" The other replied: "We are going hunting for antelope. If we kill the big variety, we will take it as a sign that God wants us to follow the big religion. If we kill the smaller one, then God wants us to follow the Jesus way."

They took different tracks and agreed to meet at a point further ahead. When they met, they found that they had both killed the smaller antelope. They became Christians and one of them was baptized as Levi. He became my main translation helper and my right-hand man for thirty years.

Meanwhile at Segbana, it was time for the first Boko baptisms, just three months after my arrival. That was exciting. Bob had been nurturing this group for some years, but he had a problem. The leader of the group and my helper Isifu both had two wives. Bob asked my opinion about baptizing polygamists and when he found that we were agreed, we went ahead with the baptism of twelve Bokos, including the two polygamists. After the Sunday morning church service, the eighty people who attended filed through the village singing hymns on their way to the river a mile away. We weaved our way down a narrow path through three-meter-high grass. Bob baptized them in the river and gave them Christian names, then we returned to Segbana under a blazing sun. Sarah was the only woman, Abraham the oldest member. Daniel was a leper, David the leader. Luke, Mark and Paul were the young guns. Isifu's name changed to Joseph, Thomas was the only one coming from another village.

That night we all gathered at David's compound and ten men from Bobena joined us. After eating, eight of those baptized gave their testimonies. All of them saw this step of baptism as a seal on their decision to follow Christ. They spoke of different ways God had already helped them. Sarah had prayed for a daughter and had twin girls. Thomas was always being stung by scorpions, but not since he took the Jesus' way. Daniel was always good for a drink, but now had found a better way. There was a bit of disturbance from Muslims who were looking on, and then a man from Bobena stood up and told of his conversion from Islam to faith in Christ. He found the Jesus way to be sincere, where one worships God in spirit and truth. The following month three elders were appointed, followed by the Lord's Supper, and so the first Boko church was established.

In December we went to Saonzi again with several Bobena Christians. This time the crowd numbered 150. Today Saonzi is regarded as a Christian village as half the population have become Christians. It is no use getting discouraged when things look bad. At one time some preachers went to Saonzi from Bobena and came back with the following report: "We are not getting many people any more. They say our message is no good. They say Jesus' word is useless. Jesus is not God's Son; he died. If he was God's Son, he would not have died. They will not build a church this year; they are drinking beer, playing cards and other games. They are laughing and talking loudly."

Meanwhile at Bobena, the youth cleared a plot of land where they were going to build a new house for me. Bandanki had said: "Why have two missionaries in the one place. If you agree to live at Bobena, we will build a house for you." All the men joined in the work, whether Christian, Muslim or animist, and I moved into my new home in March. I was happy to be living in a Boko village, in a house where people felt free to come and greet or talk to me at any time. My house was on the river side of town where the night temperature was a little cooler. The river was small, a stream really, but it had a large gallery of trees and jungle on both sides, where there were many birds and some monkeys. Most of the streams in the Boko area are small and nearly dry up in the dry season. Even so, there was enough moisture there to support small banana plantations.

I never realized how impatient I was until I began teaching older men to read, and when people began to give me no privacy at all. Because I was a second born boy in my family I was called 'Sabi'. This name has many variations: Sai, Sale, Sae, Saale, and Se. Naturally, there are many people called Sabi, and they have to be differentiated, so people are called Short Sabi, Tall Sabi, Black Sabi, Red Sabi, and many other combinations. I was differentiated by adding the name of the village. To this day all the Boko people know me as Sabi Bobena, or Se Boena. The people also gave me a nickname, 'tawaana' which means 'fast walker'.

There were about fifty-thousand Boko in Dahomey at this time, with another 15,000 over the border in Nigeria. Within a year of my arrival among the Bokos, there were groups in five villages wanting to build churches. For that to happen, they needed encouraging regular visits, accompanied by literacy classes and some medical work. My pharmacy training was a great asset in this situation. Bob Blaschke came to the Boko area in 1953 and originally got around on horseback as there were no decent roads. His patience was now bearing fruit.

Thomas was from the village of Kambara and was the first Boko to have a Christian wedding. The traditional Boko ceremony began when the friends of a bridegroom went and carried away the prospective wife to the house of the groom. She was probably aware that her father had been receiving dowry for her, but she may never have seen him. The dowry is usually paid for several years and includes an annual gift of farm produce and a monetary gift at festivals. So, at thirteen or fourteen years of age she is suddenly kidnapped and taken to the man's house where she is bathed by the women there and later joined by some girlfriends. The morning after the kidnap, if she accepts her fate, she will sweep her husband's courtyard.

Thomas' wedding was similar, but Christianized. His father had been giving gifts for three different girls for quite a while, but as a result of prayer and Thomas' firm stand on the issue, his father honored his son's wish to have only one wife. Thomas and his fiancée had never seen each other. On the appointed day she walked six miles from her village with all her earthly possessions in a calabash on her head accompanied by several girlfriends. At nine p.m. she was kidnapped, although on this occasion she knew what was going to happen. Forty people walked to the house where she was staying, and she was handed over to Sarah, the only baptized Boko woman. Then we all walked to Thomas' house singing the following song in Boko:

> We are praying for you, Jesus will make it possible.
> As you know well, wife-taking is God's affair.
> As you know well, husband-making is God's affair.
> As you know well, having children is God's affair.
> In the future may God reward you.

Bob spoke as Thomas and his bride sat together out in front, and she consented to the questions even though she had had no Christian teaching yet. As the Boko church was being established it was a problem that there were many Christian men, but no committed girls. Some young men were discouraged by rumors that if they became Christians, they wouldn't get a wife. And there were some fathers who didn't want to give their daughters to Christians. However, the custom was for a girl to follow her husband's religion, so most of them found faith in Christ in due time.

Back at Bobena, I organized for David to come and dig a well in the center of the village. This was in response to the people of Bobena building me a house. Until that time, they had bathed in and drawn their drinking water from the same places in the local stream, and where pigs sometimes wallowed.

In April 1970, the Blaschkes moved 440 miles away to Cotonou, the main city in Benin, and they were to be away for two years. I was now on my own, but not lonely. A new work began at Serekibe six miles from Bobena. David from Segbana started preaching there. He was the most outgoing and spiritual of the Boko Christians and also a composer of Christian songs. We only had fifteen songs, so I encouraged him to compose some more by giving him translations of some English hymns and singing him the tunes. Eventually he was able to compose his own words with more authentic Boko tunes. Music was an important part of church life and it was important that the songs reflected their own sense of poetry, and that the tunes agreed with the tones on the words. You can't finish a line on a high note, if the tone on the last syllable of the word is low. We had a problem with the musical instruments also. They were all dedicated to the bush spirits when they were made, because traditional Boko music was all for the praise of bush spirits that they used to sacrifice to and worship. The Boko Christians didn't feel it was appropriate to use them in Christian worship. So, they used sticks and triangles and calabashes and a piano accordion until such time as they could make their own drums and acquire guitars and keyboards.

Bob and Carol-Lee Blaschke and family (1973)

I began literacy classes at Serekibe and was overwhelmed with the number wanting to learn. Thirty-five men and ten boys bought reading primers. I travelled to Serekibe on my motor scooter each Sunday and stayed until Tuesday. Sunday evening before sunset we had a literacy class, and then after eating, we had a gospel meeting. Someone would read a story about Jesus and then preach a little, and I added a few semi-comprehensible remarks in my halting Boko. At Monday daybreak we had another literacy class and then the same program on Monday evening and Tuesday morning. Six meetings each week in addition to David's preaching on Sunday morning. At all the meetings they would sing Christian songs and pray and were encouraged to follow Jesus. Many dropped away over time, and sometimes churches closed down for a time, but this is how our Boko churches got started.

We planned a baptismal service for Bobena in September 1970. With my limited knowledge of Boko, I carefully translated one hundred key New Testament verses which were used in the lessons. I read the lessons and had a Boko repeat all that I said. The day before the baptisms, thirty Christians had come from four villages to witness the occasion. I had twenty visitors sleeping in my front room. Although there were not many Christian women at Bobena, many women came and helped prepare food and the men and boys from the church donated a chicken each. After the church service we all walked down to the river where eighteen people were baptized, four men, two women and twelve teenage boys. A big disappointment was that two men, including the village chief, pulled out within twenty-four hours of the baptism. There were many rumors and threats going around to discourage those being baptized. Relatives came from other villages to talk them out of it. One rumor that caused some anxiety was that Christians can't have more than four children! During the festivities I cooked rice for one hundred. Unfortunately, it ended up burnt, uncooked, too salty and with stones in it. Nevertheless, it was all eaten up.

Literacy programs were going strong in three villages, and in 1971 we started teaching literacy and preaching in three more villages. Two hundred copies of reading primers number one and two were duplicated at Bobena, then folded and stapled together. It was very frustrating duplicating booklets before the days of photocopiers. Many pages were wasted because of crooked lines, smudging and fading. In those days we used a mimeograph machine and a typed stencil.

I bought a second-hand Land Rover from an Australian missionary doctor named Ken Elliott who was moving to a remote area in Burkina Faso. Many years later he was kidnapped by terrorists, and at the time of writing, he has still not been released. It was a great improvement on the bicycle I had started off with, and the motor scooter that followed. Following is a description of a typical Sunday.

After church in Bobena I prepared to go away for the day with David. Boys pushed us off because the battery was flat. On the way the makeshift fan belt which was made from a bowstring broke twice. At Serebani the men were busy digging a well, so we told them we would return in the evening. At Serekibe the Christians were waiting for us; they no longer work on their farms on Sundays. Forty attended the service and afterwards, I sold some booklets and medicines and then chose nine men to accompany us to Gbarana. At Gbarana we were greeted enthusiastically and after greeting the chief we went to see the progress on their new church. The walls were about three feet high. We sold twenty-eight reading primers, medicines, pens and exercise books. Then we had a service under a shady tree where two of the men preached. Then we were all fed with pounded yam and antelope.

I was called to see a sick baby, and then we left Gbarana for Poueyla. On entering the village, we saw the leader of the Christian group sitting by the mosque doing his ablutions. He had become a Muslim six days before. We met with the others and appointed a new leader. (The following year he realized his mistake and left Islam and came back to Christ.) Then we went on to Serebani where we met for another service. After dropping off the Serekibe people, David and I started the eight-mile journey home. As darkness descended the fan belt came off several times and we finally replaced it with a rope. We arrived home at 8:30 p.m. tired and hungry, but we praised the Lord for another opportunity to visit these villages which have so recently been reached with the gospel.

During the month of May I visited over twenty Boko villages, many for the first time. May is part of the hot season, when the daily temperature reaches 35-40°. We had fair to good crowds wherever we went. What would be the future for these villages? Who can go and teach all these people? In seemed such a challenge, but praise God before I left Dahomey that year six churches had been established, and today nearly all these villages have a church and pastor.

On one occasion I wanted to visit the village of Lugu, some twenty miles away with some helpers. The Land Rover had a problem and so we set out on bicycle. When we reached the village of Senwa, I was feeling weak and feverish. I had malaria. They found me a hut to lie down in, and I spent the night there. I wasn't alone. There were mosquitoes flying around me. I could hear termites eating the wood in the ceiling above me, and there were mice running around on the floor. Next morning, I felt better, and we went on to Lugu where we met with the new Christians there. But in the evening, I was weak and feverish again, so we slept there.

Next morning, I felt good again and I desperately wanted to visit Zondji before returning home. I don't know how I made it home. The sun was hot overhead, the roads were sandy, making bicycle riding difficult, and I wasn't feeling good. The first thing I did on arriving home was to take my temperature; it was 106° F, 41° C. I had a little kerosene refrigerator, so I immediately got some ice out and rubbed it all over my head. Then I took some anti-malarial drugs. Fortunately, I survived.

Marriage

February 5th, 1972

**Ross and Joy with best man Len Pearce,
bridesmaid Barbara Allison,
and flower girls Anna Stewart and Robin Wrigley**

I was thirty years old and feeling the need of a wife. Joy and I had corresponded ever since I left Australia. She was now at Bible School in New Zealand. Was it God's will for me to propose to her at this time? I asked God for a sign, but nothing came. Finally, I decided that sometimes you just have to use your sanctified common sense and take the plunge. I had peace about it. My main concern was that nothing should hinder me from fulfilling the work that God had called me to among the Boko in Dahomey. I wrote a letter of proposal to Joy telling her that I loved her and felt she was just the right girl for me. I explained that I had work to do in Dahomey as she well knew, and that if she agreed to marry me, it would involve spending considerable time together as missionaries in Africa.

During the following week I had three little confirmations that my proposal to Joy was right. In a letter I received from an older lady who prayed for me regularly, she said: "Each time I receive your Dahomey Diary, I go through it to see if there is any news of an engagement." Another friend wrote and said it was time I got married.

Joy responded positively and after being accepted by SIM we were officially engaged on May 13th, 1970. She was studying for a Bachelor of Divinity degree and was a senior student at the New Zealand Bible Training Institute. She was a school teacher and while in training she gained a Bachelor of Arts degree in which she majored in French, which was to be a great asset in Dahomey.

How was I to give her an engagement ring? It was a bit hard when I was living on the other side of the world. Joy was going home to Melbourne for Christmas, so I asked my father to help out. Joy phoned him, and he told her to go to Dunklings jewelers and choose a nice engagement ring for herself up to the value of $200. Not a small sum in 1971! Joy did just that, but when she returned to New Zealand, she couldn't let out the secret until she had been accepted as a missionary by SIM. So, she used to put the ring on her finger for a while when she was studying in her room alone, and then try and get it off quickly when someone came.

I flew from Dahomey to New York in November, where I spent a few days with the Blaschkes. Then I flew to New Zealand and met Joy in Auckland. The next day we attended her graduation. We needed a few days to get reacquainted and we did so while Joy drove me around to see some of the sights in the north island of New Zealand. Then we flew home to Australia together and were reunited with our families.

In December, I was staying with Joy's family in East Bentleigh and had been feeling tired for a couple of weeks. All I could do was watch Tarzan films on the television. On Christmas eve my eyes turned yellow and we called the doctor. I was diagnosed as having hepatitis and was whisked off to Fairfield Infectious Diseases Hospital. It was a disappointment after being away from home for four Christmases, but I ate up everyone's egg and bacon each morning and made a quick and full recovery. I was out after two weeks.

The wedding was on February 5ᵗʰ at Murrumbeena Baptist Church. It was a beautiful day and the bride was radiant. Rev. Max Kingdom married us, and Joy's father assisted in the service. We had one hundred guests at Merrimu reception center in Chadstone. The temperature was over 40° and the air-conditioning was on the blink, but we didn't care.

Dad lent me his Humber Snipe and we had a happy and lovely honeymoon driving up the coast from Melbourne to Surfers Paradise and back. Can you picture us sitting on a rug in a grassy field eating prawns and chips? Or swimming at the many beaches we visited? Or watching Fiddler on the Roof at a theatre somewhere?

Then we had to travel around to report to my supporters and to raise support for Joy. At Easter we were at the Belgrave Heights Christian convention in the Dandenong Ranges east of Melbourne, missionary guests at the Campaigners for Christ camp with eighty young people.

We were farewelled at Murrumbeena Baptist Church, and we flew to Rome for our second honeymoon. From Rome we took the train to Florence, and then on to Lausanne in Switzerland, and then on to Paris and London. It was a lovely time, but Joy was pregnant

and had some morning sickness. At Lausanne, we stayed at the
Beatenberg Bible Institute. I don't remember much about it except
that the beds were very comfortable with soft eiderdowns, and there
was a beautifully illustrated text for each guest placed on the pillow.
My text was from Isaiah 43:2. It read:

> When you pass through the waters,
>   I will be with you,
> and when you pass through the rivers,
>   they shall not sweep over you.
> When you walk through the fire,
>   you will not be burned;
> the flames will not set you ablaze.

I wondered what significance that might have for me and kept
the card. It was to prove very significant.

We arrived back at our home in Bobena in June just in time for
the rainy season. It was going to be a challenge for Joy to settle down
in this new environment. She was newly married and pregnant, she
had a new language and culture to learn, and poverty and suffering
to come to terms with. Our house was humble and not very private.
One day, early one morning, a woman walked into our bedroom.
"Get out" Joy cried. "I came to give this dead mouse to your cat" was
the meek reply.

ATTACKED BY PARALYSIS

May 28th, 1973

Ross, Joy and Andrew in London

Christians in four more villages were in the process of building churches, Bob restarted the Boko Bible School at Segbana with a dozen students, and I was seriously getting into Bible translation. Everything was going well and then on May 28th 1973, the attack came.

The first sign that something was wrong was when I felt a slight constriction in my throat, and I had restricted vision when I looked to the side. The next morning, I couldn't swallow my porridge, and speech was difficult. Both Joy and I were concerned about these unusual symptoms. We sent a note to Bob at Segbana. He immediately came down to see me and decided that we should go to see a doctor, the nearest one being at our mission hospital at Bembereke 125 miles away. The doctor did some tests, but he was puzzled. In the next few days speech and swallowing became increasingly difficult until I could not swallow anything. My arms and legs were getting weaker too and the diagnosis was that I had food poisoning, or maybe polio.

On Friday morning I was driven 150 miles to an airstrip at Gurai in Nigeria where they radioed SIM leadership in Jos and asked for a SIM light aircraft to come and take me to the hospital there. I heard them saying "medical emergency, medical emergency", and my optimism dropped a notch. Joy and Andrew accompanied me. At this stage I could no longer walk. I was admitted to Evangel Hospital in Jos and for the next week I was fed by stomach tube. There were more tests including an epidural. The mission really looked after me wonderfully.

The paralysis continued to get worse. Now I could no longer turn over in bed or lift my arms or legs. I couldn't grip the doctor's hand and excess saliva was causing great discomfort. I had no pain or nausea, except for one night when my weakened condition brought on a malarial attack. I thought I had the DTs (delirium tremens). I remember lying on my back and feeling that I was about to vomit. I couldn't move, and it came up with a whoosh and went everywhere. After that I was not left in the room alone. I didn't like the tube up my nose all the time, and I somehow communicated to the medical staff to just put it in for feeding. It was feared that my lungs would become paralyzed and there were no iron lungs in Nigeria. By Sunday Joy and the doctors feared I would die. They diagnosed it as polio, but some of the symptoms baffled them. On Monday they started making arrangements to airlift me to London. That was a big decision, as I would have to be on a stretcher, and that would take up nine seats. The expense was going to be considerable. There was a lot of red tape involved and unfortunately our passports had to be retrieved from Cotonou in Dahomey.

When the doctor came and sat on my bed and told me the news that I would be airlifted to London, my heart dropped. I am an extremely optimistic person, and for the first time I realized the gravity of the current situation. A tear escaped from my eye. Joy of course was more distressed. She was staying with a New Zealand couple who were a great comfort to her.

On the way to the airport I was on a stretcher in the back of a station wagon. We went around a corner too fast, and I rolled off the stretcher and under the back seat. I cried out: "Ah! Ah!" which was the only sound I could muster. The driver stopped, and I was made more secure. A doctor and nurse were to accompany me to London together with Joy and little Andrew, who was only seven months old and didn't understand the drama that was unfolding. As we flew over the Sahara Desert, one of our group was drinking some ginger ale on the plane, and I indicated I would like to try and get a drop down my throat. I succeeded in swallowing a drop or two and felt that my condition might be improving.

We flew from Kano in Nigeria to London via Rome. It was Derby day. At London, an ambulance was waiting and took us to the London Hospital. The doctor and I were in the back together with an ambulance attendant. I couldn't talk, but the doctor was chatting with the attendant who had short hair and dressed in a uniform and tie. I realized that it was a woman, but I could tell by the doctor's questions that he was under the impression that it was a man. He finally said: "And what does your wife do?" After a bit of confusion my eyes lit up as I tried to rectify the situation mumbling: "I knew, I knew." She said, "I know you did".

At midnight we arrived at the hospital and a doctor rushed down the stairs and said to me: "Are you the one with ascending myelitis?" I couldn't talk, and I had never heard the expression. Then my doctor introduced himself. As soon as I arrived in England, I felt a bit better and within two days I could swallow some saliva. Fortunately, in the rush I had been admitted to London Hospital, which is a National Health Service hospital, and I was told I would not have to pay any hospital or medical fees. The doctors did lots of tests and initially concluded that I had Guillain Barré Syndrome, which is a paralysis that follows sometime after a viral infection. One of the neurologists asked me if I would mind being taken down to the basement to be shown to a class of fourth year medical students, as this condition was quite rare. After talking to the students about the condition, he removed the blanket from one leg and said that I would have no reflexes for up to six months. He tapped my leg just below the knee and was completely taken aback when my leg responded. He immediately replaced the blanket and changed his diagnosis to botulism, but no laboratory evidence was found, and other doctors weren't convinced. I told them hundreds of people all around the world were praying for me and perhaps that is why I had made a quick recovery. They still weren't convinced. One day a specialist came and sat by my bedside and said he was going to ask me three questions. One question was: "Have you eaten a chicken that might have eaten moldy grain?" To that I answered yes, and that was their final diagnosis. I had chickens at Bobena, and I fed them maize from a 55-gallon drum. I noticed one day that some moisture had condensed inside the drum and had caused some of the grain to sprout and become moldy, but I had not thought any more about it. However, the story does not end there.

Joy and Andrew had been coming by train each day to visit me. We were very thankful to SIM for their caring attitude and willingness to do all possible to save my life, despite the expense. We were also very thankful to the whole SIM family and our supporters back home. Details of my situation had been sent to SIM offices all over the world and disseminated as an urgent prayer request. People prayed and God in his faithfulness answered. Supporters back home in Australia sent in gifts towards the cost of my evacuation, and everything was covered.

I stopped tube feeding soon after arriving in London and then I started walking again, and the saliva problem was gradually improving. I could eat solids again if they weren't too dry. The only real pain I had through the whole ordeal was when impacted feces were extracted by hand at the London hospital. I had been told earlier that I might not be able to produce children again, but now the doctors expected a one-hundred percent recovery.

When I left hospital, the doctors recommended two month's convalescence in a cool climate before returning to Africa. I still had blurred vision when I looked to the side, I had difficulty swallowing some foods, and it was a struggle to walk up stairs. SIM provided a flat for us to live in Wimbledon, and soon we were making trips into London.

The first Sunday out of hospital, we went to church and the preacher referred to Isaiah 43:2: "When you pass through the waters, I will be with you". That was the first time that I remembered that the Lord had given me that verse in Beatenberg nearly one year back. The Lord had forewarned, but I had forgotten. He had indeed been with me, and protected me, and rescued me from the dangerous condition I had been in. While in UK Andrew was making good progress. He had learnt to sit and crawl and was the proud owner of three teeth. Before we left UK, we had a week's holiday on the Isle of Wight and then we attended the deeper life Christian convention at Keswick and had a few days in Scotland.

On arriving back at Bobena in August we were given an enthusiastic welcome, especially as Muslims had spread the rumor that I was dead. I even had some people playfully throwing stones at me, which is a custom they have when someone is seen alive who was thought to be dead. Just to make sure I was flesh and bone.

I soon heard rumors that a witchdoctor, or sorcerer, who lived in a village just a couple of miles from Bobena, had made claims that it was he who made me sick. In Boko animistic society it is common for people to curse each other, and it is staunchly believed that sorcerers can make people sick or cause them to die through their magical arts. They can also heal people by neutralizing another person's curse. I never confronted him about it, but I heard that he was upset that so many people he had cursed had come to our dispensary and been healed. So he said: "If this white man is healing people whom I have cursed, then I will put a curse on him." I believe it is possible, but on the whole, I have found that the Christian Boko are immune to these curses which so often affect both animists and Muslims. Even Muslims have their own sorcerers and every year we would hear stories of people dying mysteriously through sorcery. On the other hand, I was not completely convinced that my sickness came through eating a chicken that had eaten moldy grain. Why was it that no one else was affected? I do believe it was a Satanic attack, whatever the cause, and prayer gained the victory.

There were several other drawbacks to our work at this time. On arriving back at Bobena we found that no less than three of the Christians had been involved in immorality. T. was leading the literacy classes; another was our houseboy and the third was a translation helper. They had all played up during this sinister time. They had all slept with young married girls who were living at Bobena, away from their husbands at the time. T. came and confessed two days after we arrived home. He had impregnated a girl who was twenty years old and had already been married twice. He didn't want to marry her but according to custom couldn't sever relations with her until the baby was born. She had also threatened to abort the child if he rejected her. After several weeks the elders of the church and I had another talk with him, and he decided to break the relationship and trust in Jesus for the outcome. The Christians were at the stage where they were learning that Christianity is not just living socially acceptable lives, but following Jesus even when it was not socially acceptable. In problems involving immorality or sorcery it is difficult for the foreign missionary to understand the social mores and pressures, and so we had to rely a lot on the counsel of newly-elected church elders.

Then Bandanki found a letter addressed to me in his house. The letter accused both my houseboy and translation helper of adultery. "You have come to teach us God's word" the letter said, "but your workers are spoiling our stomachs." The letter was presumably written in another village by one of the jilted husbands. The houseboy and translation helper both admitted to having sinned and confessed in church publicly. I could not bear the thought of dismissing these boys whom I loved and had trained over many months. But both of them came from other villages, and the Christians at Bobena did not accept their apology or confession. They said: "They only confessed because they want to keep their jobs. They have come to this village and spoilt the name of the Bobena Christians."

We put the matter to a church vote, and they voted against me re-employing them. This was a real blow, but we hoped this disciplinary action would be a warning to all the Boko Christians. I re-employed them after some time, but in the long run neither of them recovered from their bad behavior. The houseboy could not give up his girl. He eventually married her (called "wife stealing") and became a Muslim. The translation helper's friend bore him a child, but he never married and has been a loner ever since.

Another discouragement at this time was a letter from Serekibe. It said that only seven of the twenty-one baptized Christians were serious. The others came to church irregularly and were following worldly pursuits. Just as the birth of a baby is a struggle with many pains, so it was with many of the Boko churches. But they do survive. Joy had a second attack of bacillary dysentery at this time, which laid her low for several days. There were many tropical diseases to which our bodies had low resistance.

In November we were on our way home from shopping for supplies in Parakou and having extensive mechanical work done on our Land Rover. We had a heavy load and the roads were rough. At nine p.m. while climbing a very steep hill, a back-axle shaft broke. I walked back to the last village where I found nine men who came and pushed us up to the top of the hill. Thanks to the four-wheel drive, we were able to continue our journey to Bobena. Joy patiently endured while, Andrew was scared of the revving of the motor and the darkness outside.

By the end of the year things were looking better. The gospel of John had been translated and the gospel of Mark was duplicated at Segbana. In November, seventeen Christians were baptized at Gbarana, and in December, twenty-four people were baptized at Saonzi. We now had baptized church communities in five villages, and churches built in two more. And more villages were showing interest in learning about Jesus.

The Saonzi baptisms took place on Christmas day and in the evening a cow was killed as we gathered for a feast. We wanted to put Christmas on the calendar in this remote area, as many Christians, let alone other people, knew nothing about Christmas.

Funerals, Spirits, Sorcery and Sacrifice

A Boko grave with the body lying under the wood

When the oldest inhabitant of Bobena died, messengers were sent off to the neighboring villages on bicycles, so that representatives could come and witness the burial. Usually the dead are buried as soon as the grave can be dug, but Gemblaaten was over one hundred years old, and he wasn't buried until six hours later. He was already married when the French first arrived in the area in 1890. Some of his children who attended the funeral were in their seventies.

He died at seven a.m. and soon after guns were fired to announce a death in the village. The older women wrapped his body in their cloths and carried it around the village wrapped in a mat. They stopped every now and again and danced, and then laid their hands on his body. They were paying their last respects. After an older person has died, most of the ritual is done to stop the dead person's spirit from bothering the living, especially relatives.

Crowds of people were around as the grave was being dug. Drums were being beaten, African violins made of gourd, lizard skin and horse hair were making a screeching sound, and a sixty-year-old grand-daughter was jumping around and throwing her arms about in mock sorrow. All the men sat around chatting to each other and sipping the occasional beer, but nobody would eat until the body was buried. They said it is not sad when an old person dies, but we saw tears in the eyes of a seventy-five-year-old son. Guns fired periodically, and whenever a delegation arrived from another village, the women would bring out the wrapped-up corpse on their heads and put it down before them.

When the grave was finally finished, the body was stripped of rings and other ornaments, and it was wrapped in just one cloth and lowered on a mat into the five-foot-deep grave. Someone threw some tobacco into the grave and said: "Here's your tobacco. Don't come back looking for it." Someone else put an egg in and said: "Here are your children. Don't come back bothering them." In a similar fashion a cola nut and some soap were dropped in. Then wooden slats were laid five cm above the body on a ledge that had been cut into the sides of the grave. The slats were covered with grass and then with mud, in a way that no soil fell on the body. Relatives threw the first sand in, and then the grave was filled in. When the grave was half full and again when it was full, a man with a live rooster and a bunch of ebony leaves in his hand walked all over the grave and rubbed the rooster and leaves all over it. Most young people no longer know the reason for these rituals. Ebony leaves are a symbol of courage, and the rooster serves to remove the defilement from the gravediggers.

Every now and again the women would ululate and cry out: "There are stones in the road, there are roots in the road. May God give you a good resting-place." In their belief, God holds the keys to paradise, so that was a good evangelistic tool.

~

With a few fellow Christians, I went to visit an inaccessible and backward village called Doueyla. Until a couple of years ago the inhabitants of this village feared the use of any lights at night except a torch made of grass. This was because of a fetish that lived near their village called Biomo. Biomo consists of a little mud and grass hut out in the bush and it is believed that a leopard lives in it. Only the fetish priest can go inside.

A fetish is defined as an inanimate object worshipped for its supposed magical powers, or as being inhabited by a spirit. In traditional Boko belief, a fetish is a spirit that inhabits a sacred tree or rock or another sacred place. They worship these spirits via the fetish priest who will offer a sacrifice and make an incantation at the sacred place. The Boko use the same word for these bush spirits as they do for spirits who possess people.

When a Boko fetishist or animist needs guidance or protection or better health, he will go to a diviner, a person who discovers things by guessing, intuition, inspiration or magic. This may be in relation to a birth, marriage, death, bad health, bad omen or a curse. After divining with stones, or sand, or the entrails of an animal, he will tell the enquirer what he has to do. Usually it will require that the enquirer makes a sacrifice to his personal fetish, and the diviner will tell the enquirer to go to the fetish priest with a black chicken, a white goat or whatever. He may have to travel a considerable distance to find the priest who will take him to where the fetish resides. The priest kills the offering, spatters some blood at the sacred place and maybe puts some feathers in the blood. Then he makes his sacred incantation which is the most important part of the ritual; a request to help the cause of the enquirer. The priest gets some or all of the meat for his efforts, and sometimes other gifts as well. The enquirer goes home in peace, knowing that he has done all that was possible to procure a good outcome.

So, when we entered the village of Doueyla, we knew what controlled these people's minds. We told them that if they put their faith in Jesus, they would not need to fear death, sickness or evil omens. God would love them and look after them. Many of them asked what their attitude to Biomo should be, if they followed Jesus. We told them that we knew of no other authority but Jesus in spiritual matters. They were concerned about a backlash if they turned their backs on Biomo. Eight people came that night and said they wanted to follow Jesus.

The house we were to stay was filled with cockroaches and mice, so we slept under the stars. Even there a mouse ran over my foot on two occasions. On the way home we saw many baboons, several monkeys and an antelope. We turned off the road and went down to a river where we had heard there were hippopotami, but the undergrowth was so thick that we couldn't see them, and that was frustrating. We could hear the hippos grunting and splashing around in the water, but we couldn't get close. Bush animals are rarely seen in the Boko area now; they are the victims of hunting with guns and spreading civilization.

~

One day while translating, a Fulani man came in for medicine. The Fulani are cattle herders and they live in encampments in close proximity to all the Boko villages. He said a spider had bitten him about two months ago and now he had a dry peeling rash all over his body. I consulted my books, but they didn't say anything about spiders causing rashes. After several questions I asked whether the spider was a big one or a small one. "Oh, we didn't see a spider, but somebody said that a spider must have caused it," he said.

When children get convulsions with meningitis, the mothers will say that a rabbit has caught the child. The porcupine causes other symptoms. If we suggest that flies and mosquitoes are the real culprits, they think we are as silly as we think they are.

Many accidents occur in farming communities. People stub their toes on rocks or roots, or slash open a foot with a hoe or an axe. Pieces of wood often penetrate the flesh. Then there are the primitive guns. One day a young man came in with a mashed-up eyeball. The bolt of his gun had backfired into his face. Another day we removed a three-inch piece of gun mechanism from a man's hand. He didn't have any broken bones. Another old man fell into the fire at night. His thigh healed up nicely, but all four fingers of his left hand were burnt through to the bone and it took some months for the flesh to close over them again. We treated on average one person a week for scorpion stings.

Filaria, malaria, gonorrhea, amoebic and bacillary dysenteries, eye infections, back pain, tropical ulcers, abscesses, pneumonia, coughs and colds are all common diseases we had to treat. We used to have ten to twenty patients a day and when I went on evangelistic trips on Sundays, people would flock to me to buy medicines. We bought medicines cheaply from the mission hospital and sold them cheaply to the people without profit. It was a labor of love. Joy was a trained teacher, but I taught her how to treat all these ailments. Then she ran the dispensary for a couple of hours each day, enabling me to get on with my translation work.

Sick children are the saddest cases. One month they are fat and the next month they are skin and bone, due to diarrhea, malaria or bronchial problems. Others suffer from malnutrition and swell up. Now and then a measles epidemic would sweep through the area, killing quite a few children. Married women tried to have a baby every four years, after weaning the previous one, but half of the babies died in their infancy. Some had ten children, but today with mandatory education, six children are enough.

The most frustrating aspect of the medical work was that people come too late, often fatalistically. They say: "I left it with God." Yapenu used to come to church for a while. Then she got an eye infection. She came and bought eye ointment a couple of times, and then we didn't see her any more. When we did catch up with her, she was blind. However, thank God, she now has spiritual sight. We prepared a couple of health booklets in Boko called: 'Good health' and 'Flies are your enemies'.

Sarah and her twin daughters

The first Boko woman to be baptized had died. We had taken Sarah to the mission hospital, only to find out that she had inoperable cancer. After returning to Segbana she was only able to make it to one Sunday service, but there was a steady stream of Christians going to visit her. Her twin daughters were about to be married and she was able to attend the first wedding, but not the second one a week later.

In death, as throughout her Christian life, there was a clash between tradition and the Christian faith. Boko people are born either as peasants or lords. It doesn't make much difference in life any more, but when they die, peasants are wrapped in black cloth and buried with their legs doubled back. If you are not buried in the correct way, your ancestors won't recognize you, and they will reject you. What could be worse than being rejected by the spirits of your ancestors? You are left to wander alone forever.

When Sarah died, the Christians made sure they had charge of her body for burial. They decided that a saint should be buried in white cloth not black, and with the body straight, not crooked. The unbelievers were horrified and frightened that Sarah's spirit would return to bother them for burying her the wrong way.

Sarah had been a Christian for fifteen years. Before that she was a nominal Muslim, but she longed for eternal life. When Bob came to her village and said: "Who wants eternal life?" she was all ears. When she had twins, her husband wanted her to get rid of the defilement by sleeping with another man before she came back to him. Sarah refused and went to live in Segbana where she could attend church. She had twins again by her third husband and he eventually left her for the same reason. Boko traditions like these have caused many to fall away, but Sarah trusted the Lord and was a great example and pioneer in her new-found faith. She refused to consult diviners or mediums and would not sacrifice to fetishes. Her relatives continually pressed her with the old ways of the devil and eventually she had to leave them and start a new household. "Your household will become an ash-heap in no time," they scoffed, but soon Sarah had eight children living with her. The villagers continued to pressure her to join in their witchcraft, and when she refused, they cast spells on her. When these didn't work, they set fire to her house, but then the fire didn't take.

Sarah used to tithe all her produce, even though she had little. She stopped brewing beer when she took account of what it did to people. Even when dying she did not succumb to the temptation to offer a sacrifice. She died victoriously, leaving four out of seven Christian children. She said: "Do not mourn my death as the pagans do. Kill a cow and rejoice that I am with Jesus."

Months later her pagan relatives decided that they should have their own funeral celebration for her. A large crowd gathered and there was the usual drunkenness. The funeral was marred by fighting and by one of the children wandering off into the bush, getting lost and dying. They went to the diviner to enquire why these bad things had happened at Sarah's funeral. The pagan diviner's answer was that Sarah wanted the first funeral she had, but she didn't want the second.

~

Two Christian women got up early and went into the bush to collect shea nuts from which the local oil called 'shea-nut butter' is made. They returned at midday and went off for another load, returning again in the evening. These two saints were persecuted for what they did, and some of their fellow Christian women were the most vehement with their insults.

A spirit had decreed through a medium that women weren't to go and collect shea nuts on Fridays. If they went, they would mislay their calabashes and get lost in the bush. As there is great competition to get the nuts, these two Christians were not only defying the spirit, but they were also seen as taking advantage of the other women's fear.

This was not an isolated incident. Every year there are many decrees from spirits and all Boko women, whether Muslim or pagan, obey. With the traditional way of life being very communal in nature, it is difficult to step out and be different. Nevertheless, Christians are encouraged to be faithful to Jesus and not follow the commands of spirits.

At another time a woman died in childbirth and the message went around that women should hide from her spirit until she was buried. They all shot off into the bush to hide for the morning. On another occasion a woman died while coming home from the bush with a load of firewood. A collection was taken up and the money given to a Muslim medium, who said she would appease the spirits.

When Levi and his friend became Christians after killing the smaller antelopes, they were challenged in a similar way. A medium in their village would make an announcement each year regarding the time when people could start pounding yams for their favorite dish, pounded yam. Levi and his friend queried: "Why should we take any notice of what a medium says?" So, they decided to pound yam before the medium's announcement. The women warned them that they would die. When they didn't die, the women said that it was because they pounded the yam at the farm and not in the village. The following year they did the same thing, but this time, in the village. Nothing happened, so the women said: "It must be because you are men. If a woman did it, she would surely die."

~

Boko people are born with a taboo. If they break the taboo, they will suffer. David was among the first group baptized and was a man of great faith. His taboo was monkey. If he ate monkey, he would go blind. When the opportunity came, David, with great courage, announced that he was going to eat his taboo. Nothing happened to him. It is because of Christian testimonies like this that many of these practices and fears are dying out.

But many people still wear charms. These are usually rings, or small leather pouches worn around the neck with words of the Quran inside. A sorcerer will boil up a ring with a dead scorpion and make an incantation, and then he will sell it as a protection against scorpion stings. You can ask for a charm to protect you against curses or any concern that you have.

~

A Christian girl went to another village one day and saw someone wearing a bracelet she liked. She asked to have it and was given it. From that time on she started acting strangely. When in church, she would suddenly get up and go outside. Friends thought she was going to the toilet, but one day they went to look for her and found her lying on her back in the grass under the blazing sun. She did other strange things, like speaking in unknown languages, and eventually the church elders called her and asked her to explain her behavior. She said it all started when she started wearing her bracelet. They took it off her, burnt it in a fire and prayed for her. That was the end of her strange behavior.

~

There was a twin in a Christian household who was asked by his mother's family to go and help with some ploughing. He was about twenty. Twins are significant in animistic culture, as they are believed to have special powers. If a twin has died, a peg will be made like a quoit peg and a shirt is made with a piece of woven cloth and put on the peg. From time to time porridge is poured on it. The dead twin is being dressed and fed.

Before daybreak this twin was walking along a narrow path with two oxen which would be used for ploughing. Suddenly he saw some strange beings in the morning gloom. One of them said to the other: "Shall we kill him?" The other one replied: "No, his counterpart is back in the village." When his relatives found him, he was in a delirium, and the oxen had wandered off. Back home again, he cut himself off from people. He had a fear of people and just wanted to sit alone in his house.

A month or so later I visited his father and asked how everyone was. He said that one son wasn't well and explained what had happened. I went in to see him and found him unkempt, his house and clothes very dirty. He could talk but was not very talkative. I asked him what had happened to him and he told me some details. I assured him that Jesus could help him and asked him whether he believed Jesus could heal him, and if he would come to the Thursday night prayer meeting at the church where we would pray for him. He agreed.

Praying for him and delivering him from what we perceived as demonic oppression was our main aim that evening. Several of us prayed for him, but nothing dramatic happened. One Christian said to me: "I feel the Lord saying that he should clean himself up and that we should pray for him in his house." I told the oppressed boy and his family that they should clean up his house and wash all his clothes. He was to cut off all his matted hair and have a good bath, and we would come and pray for him again the following evening. We did that, and he was delivered and gradually reverted to a normal life. The Christians who knew about his poor condition did not have the confidence to do something about rescuing him. Maybe they feared the spirits. So this was a good lesson for them.

~

There is a 'gai' society among the Boko which consists mainly of possessed women. They wear a band around their heads as their headscarf and often have scowls on their faces. When a possessed woman dies, the family looks for women to come and inhale incense to the screech of violins until the *gai* spirit possesses one of them. Being possessed by a spirit may not be your cup of tea, but many Boko women covet the opportunity. It gives them a sense of power, and they are feared in Boko society. It is these women who act as mediums. When possessed, they can go into trances and jump around with supernatural strength. When speaking in a trance they speak in Bisã, a language spoken 125 miles away in Nigeria, and possibly the original form of Boko. One 'gai' I knew in Bobena was said to have the spirit of a hyena. Whenever she asked people for meat, they would give it to her.

One day a 'gai' died in Segbana and the next day they were to seek a candidate to take on the dead woman's spirit. The ceremony was to take place quite close to the mission compound, so I decided to go and watch the proceedings, which wasn't my usual practice. I was skeptical about some things I was told, so some Boko friends told me to come and see for myself. They said that the dead body would shake or convulse when the right candidate came forward. There were a lot of people gathered around in a circle and men were making rhythmic noises by beating large calabashes. A mortar used for pounding grain was turned upside down and propped up against the mortar was the dead woman's corpse. On the other side of the circle there were several girl candidates. The calabashes were beaten loudly, and as the girls were presented, everyone waiting expectantly for the corpse to shake. But nothing happened, and the people went home disappointed. The older women blamed the failure of the corpse to react on the pastor's presence. Me!

BIBLE TRANSLATION AND BIBLE SCHOOL

1974-1977

Early translation work at Bobena

The Boko Bible School began in July 1974. Nine men were chosen from five villages to attend. They would come to Bobena every Sunday evening and leave again on Monday evening, but later we changed this to Sunday through to Tuesday every two weeks. Some travelled twenty miles on bicycles while others walked eight miles. The program started at 6:30 a.m. with prayer and a cup of tea followed by a Bible study until nine a.m. After porridge, Joy taught them French for an hour, and after that there was preaching class and Bible exposition. In the afternoon there was reading and writing practice, followed by reading stories about Jesus and writing a summary of what they had read. We used to spend a lot of time talking about church problems and policies: polygamy, funerals, working on Sunday, sacrificing to fetishes, persecution, witnessing, reading classes and the like. The men were keen. One said he would follow Jesus even if it meant being burnt to death. Nevertheless, within six months two men had dropped out. One didn't have the potential, the other one illustrates the marriage problems that were encountered at this time.

One Monday morning during the prayer time a man rose and said he wanted to take a new wife. Everyone was surprised, as they knew that Christians don't have two wives. The man explained that he had been paying dowry for this girl for three years and she was now old enough to marry. Furthermore, his present wife was no good. She wasn't interested in becoming a Christian and she was always taking off and living in other villages for months on end. Was he to reject the girl he had been paying for and who wanted to become a Christian in preference for his present wife who was so unstable? I told him that there were only two biblical reasons for divorce, adultery and desertion. A couple of weeks later the man came and said his father-in-law had come and taken his wife away and she wouldn't be coming back. I told him to go and talk to his wife as he had married her, not the father, but he said that his wife was not independent; she belonged to the father.

So the man married his new wife. When visiting his church one day, he asked me to pray for him and his new wife. I heard that the old wife was in the village, so I went to see her and to ask what the situation was. She said she didn't know, so I went to see her father, who, as our friend had said, didn't want his daughter to be his wife any longer. So, I prayed for him and his new wife and told him not to have anything more to do with the old one. Not long after I returned to Gbarana and found him living with both wives. He was relieved of his responsibilities as church leader and pastor in training. Eventually he reverted to Islam.

Bob Blaschke came back to Segbana and led the Bible school for two years, after which it fell back into my hands. Bible school and translation work complemented each other. I would teach newly translated books to them and in the process find improvements to make to the translation.

Bible study in the bush

Sometimes I would take the Bible students for a two-day camp in the bush. I could fit a dozen men into the Land Rover with our equipment stacked on the roof rack. On one occasion we read through the newly translated Gospel of John and had good times of prayer. But on the way home two tires blew simultaneously. Both were pierced in the side by a right-angled stump of wood. Having only one spare tire, we had to walk ten miles back to Segbana to get another one.

In March 1976 we went bush for three days of relaxation: swimming in the river, hunting and fishing, interspersed with eight studies on 1 & 2 Peter. We spent one day digging up a three-meter python that was living in an aardvark's hole. David entered the large hole on his belly with a torch and could see the python. We dug a hole from the top until we reached it, only to see its tail disappearing further down the hole and winding underneath the first level. We continued digging until the python had nowhere further to go. The python steaks made it all worthwhile.

Translation of the Boko New Testament started in 1973 and the first draft was completed in late 1977. After a complete revision during 1981-83 it was published in 1984. All the books that were translated early had to be revised several times, because as the work progressed, we became more proficient and my knowledge of Boko idiom was improving all the time. My job description was linguist-exegete, which meant that it was my responsibility to make sure the grammar was correct and that our interpretation of the original Greek documents was correct. I was responsible for the accuracy of the translation. My Boko informants, or language consultants as we later called them, were responsible for ensuring that the Boko expression was clear and natural and in good Boko idiom. Before 1980 I had many informants and our work was lacking in precision and not fully idiomatic.

This is the general translation procedure we followed in 1976.

1. A Boko helper made the first draft from a French version
2. I made my own translation from the Greek with the help of an eight-translation parallel New Testament, a Greek lexicon and commentaries
3. The helper wrote his translation on the blackboard and the team went through it verse by verse making suggestions and discussing alternatives

4. Another helper typed up the corrected text from the blackboard and after I checked it, he typed up five copies. This was the second draft.

5. These copies were given to the best Bible School students to read for comprehension and style. We read it through together at Bible school and the translation team checked the suggested changes.

6. The third draft was typed up on stencils and the translation was duplicated on a mimeograph machine.

7. Young Christians would come and help me with folding the pages and compiling and stapling the booklets, which were sold to the faithful.

One of my early informants was Bani, who at baptism took the name, Amos. At the age of seventeen he clapped at my door one day and said he wanted to join my club. He meant he wanted to become a Christian. I told him about Jesus and he became a devoted follower. Every evening at six p.m. he went into the bush with his radio to listen to a Christian radio program on short wave and to pray. He knew French and so was a great asset. Later he went to university in Niamey in Niger Republic, and then he did a Master of Theology degree at Bangui in Central Africa Republic, and eventually a PhD in Theology in Canada. I was only disappointed that he didn't use his skills to help develop the Boko church.

It was also my job as linguist to finalize the writing system or script of the Boko language. This took some years and just when we thought we had it right, the government radio announced that Pastors Blaschke and Jones were doing a good work with the Boko language, but they would like us to change the script. This was their official way of telling us what we should do, (long before Donald Trump came on the scene). Changing the script meant a lot of work; we had to retype and reprint all the Boko literature we had. But what they suggested was good, because it better matched the script of other languages in the country.

I found Genesis to be a vital book in preparing the Boko people for acceptance of the gospel. Following is an article I wrote for the Creation ex nihilo magazine in March-May 1996.

As a missionary, I was preaching the Gospel in a Boko village in the Republic of Benin, in western Africa. "How many of you have sinned?" I asked. There were no takers. We had been preaching the good news; how Jesus came into the world to save sinners. But to appreciate that, these people needed to hear the bad news about sin first.

The word sinner exists in the Boko language, but they only applied it to murderers, thieves, and wife-stealers. Most Boko people consider themselves to be good, and don't appreciate their need of a Savior. We were translating the New Testament at the time, and soon realized that the Bokos needed to understand the teaching of the first five chapters of Romans; that all men are sinners, under God's condemnation, and deserving of hell. We found that the only satisfactory way to teach the Boko people about sin was to go back to Genesis and tell them the early history of man, about Adam and Eve and the Fall.

What a wealth of teaching is contained in Genesis chapters 1-11: Creation, man created good and in the image of God, man's authority over the earth, marriage, Satanic opposition, the fall into sin, God seeking man, God's curse on the earth, the reason for suffering and death, sacrifice and redemption, judgment, the origin of the nations, and the beginning of false religion.

From the moment the Boko Christians read Genesis in their own language they loved it. They took it at face value. When Genesis said God created the world in six days, they believed it. When clear statements were made about the universality of the Flood, they believed them. For these people with no pre-conceived notions, that was the most natural thing to do.

Knowing they would hear about evolution sooner or later; I began to explain the basics to them. They found it incredible that the white man, with all his knowledge, could believe they came from monkeys – such nonsense!

Their conclusions are verified by Paul's teaching in Romans 1:20-22: "For since the creation of the world God's invisible qualities – his eternal power and divine nature – have been clearly seen, being understood from what has been made, so that people are without excuse. For although they knew God, they neither glorified him as God nor gave thanks to him, but their thinking became futile and their foolish hearts were darkened. Although they claimed to be wise, they became fools."

We felt the need to publish a Boko translation of Genesis along with the New Testament because it was so fundamental, but as Genesis is the introduction, we went on to translate the whole Old Testament, to give the New Testament its necessary solid foundation.

People can't appreciate the wonder of grace, forgiveness and salvation, if they have not first learnt about God's holiness and the gravity of sin. Only when they understand this will they know their need for a Savior and appreciate what Jesus has done for them.

How instructive this approach is for our Western culture. Simultaneous with Africa and other parts of the world becoming more Christian, Western nations are becoming increasingly pagan. The new paganism is cultural Marxism, whose proponents outlaw creation and Judeo-Christian values from our schools and universities. The foundation that Genesis 1-11 provides is therefore a timelier message than ever. God is the Creator of the earth, and we are under obligation to worship him.

Communism

1974-1989

Peter, Andrew, Paul and Matthew with SIMair plane

A military regime under Matthew Kerekou took power in Dahomey in November 1972 and adopted a Marxist-Leninist policy in 1974. The government formed a political organization which became known as the Party of the People's Revolution. In 1975 the name of the country was changed to The Peoples' Republic of Benin. In 1986, President Kerekou began to modify his Marxism-Leninism and by December 1989 the ideology was officially abandoned. The name Benin comes from the name of the coastal area, the Bight of Benin, which in turn was named after an ancient kingdom in southern Nigeria.

Working as missionaries in a communist country was not easy. It just added to the many difficult conditions we worked under. The average maximum temperature from February to May is 35-40° C, the minimum 22-25° C. There was no electricity or running water in the Boko area at that time, unless you created your own. There were virtually no phones. Food was difficult to obtain except for what was grown by local farmers. The roads were atrocious, making travel slow and causing many mechanical problems and accidents. Once called 'the white man's grave', there were many nasty diseases around including smallpox, yellow fever, hepatitis, meningitis, filariasis, schistosomiasis, amoebic and bacillary dysentery, malaria, typhoid, dengue, rabies, tetanus, pneumonia, tropical ulcers, malnutrition, eye infections and river blindness. I saw people suffering from most of these diseases and had six of them myself. Having a government that was opposed to our work, rather than being supportive of it, just added to our difficulties.

In 1975 I was apprehended by soldiers while on an evangelistic trip and detained for several hours. In 1976 I drove to Lugu for the Sunday morning service and in the afternoon, we continued preparing many people for baptism. I arrived home tired at six p.m. A little later a government official from Segbana drove up to our front door and got out with several policemen armed with rifles and ammunition belts. They said that under the Marxist government, when a private citizen owns something that is needed by the Revolution, then he has to loan or give it for their use. They had urgent business in a remote village called Monrou, twenty miles way, and they needed the use of my Land Rover. After negotiations it was agreed that I would drive them there, rather than lending them the vehicle. Joy's parents were staying with us at the time, and her father Neville said he would accompany me. I told them I needed to eat first and then we got going. My father-in-law and I were in the front seat with four armed men in the back. Monrou is in a classified forest and there is a river three miles before the town with varying levels of water flowing over the road where we had to cross. I was maneuvering the vehicle through the river when we became wedged on a rock. We had to jack the vehicle up and push it over the rock before we could continue on our way. That took thirty minutes.

When we arrived in the village the armed men got out and went and arrested a man, handcuffed him and threw him in the back of the Land Rover. I felt embarrassed, because I had been to this village several times encouraging people to follow Jesus. I found out later that they understood that I had been coerced into it and didn't blame me.

On the way home, the official was looking out the window into the semi darkness for game when he saw a porcupine. He told me to stop quickly, but I didn't want to have them all fall on the floor, so I stopped gently. The official fired and missed and then accused me of not stopping quickly enough. We arrived home safely, and our wives were relieved to see us.

One day, I was running a Bible School class when a messenger came from Segbana to tell me that the government was taking over our church there for use as a secondary school until a new school could be built in the dry season. The Christians could use the church for meetings on Thursday night and Sunday mornings only. I wrote a letter to the official asking him for a definite date of leaving our building. The government had already made repairs to the floors and walls.

Early in 1977 there was an attempted coup d'état in Cotonou. As a result, we were restricted to our village for two months which meant no evangelistic trips. Then in early February I was called to

Segbana to see the local government official and the chief of police. I disliked these situations because my French wasn't great, and I had difficulty in understanding them. They told me that the empty SIM mission property and contents at Segbana had been taken over by the local revolutionary council, because the place had been abandoned. Nobody had lived there for eighteen months. I was to come back the next day to do an inventory with the police and hand over the keys. Next day, however, I objected and asked for permission to travel to Parakou to see the SIM director.

The following day four armed officials came from another place to search our house at Bobena. We didn't know who they were or where they had come from and they wouldn't tell us anything. When they arrived, I was working in my translation hut a few hundred meters away. Joy was terrified and sent someone to call me. They searched our whole house including the bedrooms and then asked about our old house. I had packed two 55-gallon drums with stuff with great care to send back to Australia including some fine English china. (Why did we bring all our wedding presents to Africa?) They looked at the drums suspiciously and asked me what was inside. Then they asked me to unpack it all. How frustrating. But we were really more concerned with our lives at this point in time. We learned later that they were police from Kandi, a town sixty miles away. We thought that all the missionaries must have had the same treatment, but it was only us. Because of the attempted coup and because we lived close to the Nigerian border, they were looking for smuggled firearms. One of the Christian women said she couldn't eat or sleep that night; she was so worried about us. As for the children, they were oblivious to the situation. While the police were searching the house, Matthew cried to be breastfed, Paul climbed through the legs of one man looking for a book, and Andrew asked us if our visitors were staying for tea.

The police returned again a month later to ask more questions about our work and our international travels, until they seemed satisfied that we were bona-fide missionaries with no political connections.

It took eleven days before I received permission to go to Parakou about the Segbana house. The SIM director and I went to see the Prefect, and we were told that they had heard of the request from Segbana and were considering it. We were told to return at the end of the week for a decision. As Joy and I had already been in Parakou for a week and knew that the local people would be worried about us, we drove the two-hundred miles home. Then I had to drive back to learn that the mission property would remain ours, but we were to repair the fire damage within two months.

A few months before this a couple of SIM missionaries were married at Kandi and they honeymooned at Segbana. I could think of a better place for a honeymoon, but just to be by themselves was enough for this couple. One day they came down to Bobena to have lunch with us. At five p.m. a messenger came from Segbana to tell us that the mission house had caught fire and flames were coming out of the roof. We immediately drove there and found that the kitchen was completely gutted and the beams under the roof were burnt. The mud walls were blackened, but otherwise unaffected. The fire had been put out by police and neighbors and all the furniture had been taken out of the house, demolishing some windows and doors in the process, as the house had been locked. We didn't complain. Next morning, we spent three hours at the police station making statements. They suggested it was deliberately lit, but we explained that a gas bottle had been leaking and when the heavy gas reached the flame of the kerosene refrigerator, there was an explosion.

Despite these hindrances, with the Lord's help the work progressed. When we went home at the end of 1977, we praised God for his protection and for strength to serve him in that unknown corner of the world. Thousands of people had been treated for all those tropical diseases, and many lives were saved. Others had been saved from pain and disfigurement from injuries and burns. Over three-hundred people from a dozen villages had been taught to read and write their own language. The translation of the New Testament into Boko was completed in September 1977 after eight years of linguistic and translation work. Genesis, Exodus and seventy Psalms had also been translated.

We had had evangelistic meetings in forty villages and towns altogether, and churches had been established in seven villages, with nine more showing interest. 130 people had been baptized and 250 Boko now called themselves Christians. A Boko Bible School was established in 1974 and by 1977 fifteen men from five villages were enrolled.

Family Life in Africa

1972-1977

Ross and Joy with Paul, Andrew and Matthew

In September 1972 our loads arrived by ship from Australia, five 55-gallon drums. We also bought a new stove and refrigerator. At this time the Blaschke family returned to Segbana, so it was good to have some close neighbors again. Before they returned our nearest white neighbors were sixty miles away.

Joy's baby was due in November and she was to have it in a missionary hospital in Nigeria six-hundred miles east of Segbana. She would have to go a month beforehand and I had to stay behind and do my work. At this time SIM had their own light aircraft, so we drove Joy sixty miles to Kandi, from where she was flown to Jos and looked after by SIM missionaries. While there she sat her final Bachelor of Divinity exams. Meanwhile I felt like a bachelor again at Bobena. On October 26th there was a coup d'état in Dahomey and on November 8th Joy gave birth to a bouncing boy, Andrew Nicholas. Two weeks later Joy and Andrew were flown direct to Segbana where an airstrip had been cleared. Many Bokos came to see the aircraft and to shout 'Barika!' Congratulations! Andrew was a beautiful child, and many came to greet him each day. On Christmas night a village feast was held in Bobena. Everyone came and brought their own food. We bought a lean cow to provide some meat and provided soft drink for all. It was a double celebration for the birth of our son Andrew and the birth of the Savior of the world.

Now that we were a family, we needed a bigger and better house which we decided to build close by our old house. We put down solid concrete foundations and ordered louver windows and doors from a good carpenter in Parakou. All the Bobena men built the mud walls and put on the grass roof at a cost of $50. A mason plastered the walls inside and out and we whitewashed them. We had a well dug in the front yard and installed a pump. Water was pumped up into two 55-gallon drums and hey presto, we had running water in the kitchen and bathroom. The new house was a winner.

Every three months we would drive two-hundred miles to Parakou to buy food supplies and catch up with some of our fellow missionaries. The roads were shocking, especially during the rainy season. Some of the missionaries were English speakers from US, UK and Canada, others were French speakers from France and Switzerland. We longed for the opportunity to speak English with someone, but Dahomey being a francophone country, we were expected to speak French in mixed gatherings. We had a spiritual conference each year, and in addition, the linguists had regular seminars where they could compare notes and learn from each other. SIM had Bible translators working in seven languages in the north of the country.

Each year we would go to the SIM Rest Home at Miango in Nigeria for a month's holiday. Miango was on a plateau where the temperature was 10° cooler. In April 1972 Joy, Andrew and I drove to an airstrip at Gurai in Nigeria where we were met by a SIM light aircraft and flown five-hundred miles to Miango. There were always lots of missionaries holidaying at Miango, and each family had their own unit with two bedrooms and a bathroom. The meals were served in a common dining room and were really good. A SIM private school, Kent Academy, was adjacent to the rest home and when our children did their primary school education there, they would live with us during our stay. There were nice walking tracks on this rocky plateau, and there were tennis courts where I used to enjoy playing with my friend Phil Short from Australia. Each year, we would have our annual medical check-ups at the city of Jos twenty miles away.

In October 1974 we flew to Jos to await the birth of our second child. This time I persuaded our director that I should accompany Joy, because I could write up the Boko grammar I had analyzed while there, and also get some advice from fellow linguists at the Wycliffe Bible Translators' base in Jos.

While we were away from Dahomey there were two tragic accidents there. Roland Pickering, one of our key missionaries to whom I had written a letter from Bible College, was killed in a road accident. And then a month later Alan Gibbs died when a goods train and the passenger train in which he was travelling collided. The train caught fire and about two-hundred people were killed. Two days of national mourning were proclaimed. Witnesses said Alan was helping people out the windows of the train, but he couldn't get out himself because of his size. He left a widow and five children.

Meanwhile back at Jos, I had the opportunity to give my testimony at the local jail. Conditions were very crowded and the only food for prisoners was what their relatives brought them. The forty-five who attended the meeting would put many church gatherings to shame with their hearty singing and spontaneous prayers. As soon as I finished my testimony they broke into the choruses, "Have you been born again?" and "The things we used to do, we will do no more."

Two-year-old Andrew developed well during our two months at Miango. He went to kindergarten most mornings which gave him the opportunity to mix with white children and improve his English. Before we arrived at Jos, he only spoke some Boko words. By the time we left he was speaking English phrases.

Our second son Paul was born on November 14th 1974. He was 8 lb 4 oz at birth and was a good baby. Two weeks later we flew back to Dahomey and had one week to prepare for our break in Australia. Before we left, we killed a cow and put on a feast for the people of our village. It was Paul's coming out party, and also a goodbye for five months.

Back in Australia we spent a couple of weeks at Maffra with my Dad who was in hospital with diabetes. He was allowed to come home for Christmas and we had a happy time together. From there we drove to Sydney and spent two weeks with Joy's parents in Manly. After that we spent three months visiting churches and supporters in NSW and Victoria reporting on our work. We had fifty meetings in all and it was a real joy to catch up with our friends and relatives. At Easter Joy spoke at two women's conventions at Belgrave Heights while Ross went to the Grampians for evangelistic meetings among the campers with his friends from Open Air Campaigners. Before leaving again for Dahomey (now Benin), our young children, Andrew and Paul, were dedicated to the Lord at Murrumbeena Baptist Church. In light of the political instability in Dahomey and the fact that we had two young children, some friends urged us to stay in Australia, but both Joy and I were sure of God's call and guidance. And despite feelings of apprehension, we knew that the Boko needed us.

By the time Andrew was three years old he was fluent in both Boko and English and could translate from one to the other without any trouble. That is the age to learn a language! He had many village playmates and loved playing with them. The Boko children had no toys except ones they made for themselves. Our boys had to wear shoes and socks when playing outside because of the prevalence of hookworm. We boiled and filtered all our water, so it was hard for our boys to understand these restrictions, when their friends didn't wear shoes and drank just any water.

Andrew absorbed Boko culture. He learnt to share everything as they do, and he learnt to spit great distances through his teeth. The Bokos don't discipline small children, whereas we believed that if you don't teach a two-year-old child who is boss, you will have a hard time from that time on. One of the hard things about living in a small village is that everyone sees what you do, and we were often misunderstood, as our standards of behavior and living were so very different.

It was hard for our boys to learn to sit still in church because of their active minds and energy levels. The African children by contrast, often had a poor diet and sat so quietly. The Boko women thought our children grew so quickly because of the medicine we gave them. We tried to teach them that it was a matter of cleanliness, good food, and fly screens. Our boys did suffer from tropical ailments from time to time, and with the mission hospital four hours away, I was very thankful for my pharmacy training. We rarely had to make emergency medical trips.

Our car problems gave us a lot of grief. Sometimes it was getting bogged or having blowouts, at other times it was mechanical problems brought about by the bad roads. On returning from Australia our Land Rover refused to go. Three months later we sold it and hired another one for five months. Later in the year we went to Cotonou on the coast and got our brand-new Land Rover out of port. Surely this would solve many of our problems, but part of the problem was that I am not in the least mechanically minded, a sad failing for someone living in such conditions.

In April 1976 with our new Land Rover, we drove six-hundred miles to Miango for our annual holiday. The first night we stayed in a game reserve in Nigeria where we saw eight elephants and many antelope of various kinds. The next day we drove through ten Boko villages we hadn't been to before and where no Christian work had ever been done. That night we slept in the Land Rover by the Niger River waiting to cross it by ferry the next morning.

That year Joy's parents came to Benin to visit us for two months. Neville was able to preach many times in several of the Boko churches, and also at Bible School. I was his interpreter. Joy's parents bought a cow for a feast for the people of Bobena who had been so kind and liberal in giving of their farm produce. In the evening everyone brought their stools into the center square and there was singing and preaching, followed by rice and beef and Kool-Aid, and finally slides and filmstrips and games. There were roars of laughter as the Bokos saw themselves on the screen which consisted of a double white sheet.

Joy was pregnant again and a month before the due date we all flew to Jos with SIMair. Joy saw the doctor for the second time this pregnancy and then weekly until Matthew was born. Meanwhile, Ross translated the first draft of Revelation, Hebrews and 2 Corinthians.

Andrew and Paul were thrilled to have a baby brother. Two days out of hospital, Joy had an attack of malaria. A house was loaned to us in Jos for a week to live in before returning to Benin, but then we learned of an attempted coup in Benin. We had to go to Miango to sit it out. A couple of days later, and with only an hour's warning, we flew back to Gurai. In Benin we learnt that there was a ban on travelling until further notice, but after three hours we were given permission to drive the seventy-five miles home to Bobena.

On our annual trip to Miango in 1977 we took two of our workers, Nicholas and Mark, who relieved Joy of the daily washing and minded the children during meal times. Unfortunately, Joy slipped over with baby Matthew and while saving him she broke the fibula in her leg just below the knee. She had her leg in plaster for the next three weeks. Then our passports became lost. They had been sent to Lagos to have Matthew put on Joy's passport. They were tracked down and sent to Jos a few days late. The envelope had our Benin address on it and was sent on a flight to Benin the next morning instead of coming to us at Miango. We were a bit nervous about driving back to Benin without our passports, but we radioed missionaries in Benin to send our passports to a Nigerian town near the border where we could pick them up.

We did not know that there had been a refinery shut-down in Nigeria and petrol was very scarce. At several towns we could not buy petrol and it was only by finding a Christian bookshop or church and asking for help that we were able to get some. We were running late and couldn't reach our destination, so at ten p.m. we set up camp in the African bush. We were tired and put the tents up quickly, Joy and Matthew and I in one, Andrew and Paul and another missionary in another, and Nicholas and Mark in the third. At midnight a fierce storm blew up and blew our tents down. Scrambling around in the rain we fixed them up, but we were in a depression and water flowed into two of them and we had to sleep in the Land Rover for the rest of the night. After breakfast we found a petrol station with petrol for the first time in five-hundred miles, but we had to wait in a queue for four hours before filling up. Further along at New Bussa the queue was a mile long and we didn't have the energy to wait it out, so we went on in faith.

The gauge had been on empty for twelve miles when we finally got a gallon of fuel in a small village. That took us to Gurai where we slept the night and were given our passports. The local pastor gave us two gallons the next morning and we finally arrived home safely that evening.

Paul had a swelling on his head which distorted his face somewhat. I diagnosed it as filaria and gave him a fraction of a tablet. This caused the white of his right eye to become edematous and then another tender spot swelled up. He soon recovered. Meanwhile Andrew had several dog hookworms crawling around under the skin of his hands and feet. They were two inches long and as thin as cotton. These came from playing in soil where a dog had urinated. Who can keep a four-year-old out of it? He was very adventurous and liked to wander off with his friends to the creek or the bush or a farm.

By the end of the year we were looking forward to some recreation time in Australia. In Benin we had neither the time nor the facilities. There was no sea to visit, or trips to the hills. No big stores to shop at, or nice places to go on picnics without flies and sweat bees and other creepy-crawlies. Nor were there chops and sausages to barbecue. Nor were there friends or relatives close by to visit. We looked forward to catching up, but we didn't know that this would be a long break from Benin.

PART 3

OVERCOMING ADVERSITY

Recuperation in Australia

1978-1980

Ross and Joy, Andrew, Matt, Pete and Paul

After the usual catching up with our families and travelling around reporting to our supporters, we went to Sydney to consult with our SIM national director. Joy had been suffering from depression for some time and it was felt that she needed more time to recuperate. Our time at home was lengthened until August, and I was appointed Victorian Representative for SIM for the remaining time in Australia.

We lived at the SIM home in Ashburton where Andrew started attending primary school. Matthew started walking in March and continued to have breath-holding fits. His body would suddenly go stiff and he couldn't breathe, and his eyes would roll back in his head. The doctor said he would grow out of it. We had got used to them, but not others. One Sunday I was preaching at a German Baptist church and Matthew was in the crèche. Suddenly the lady in charge came running down the aisle asking me to come quickly. I told her not to worry, and Joy went to help out.

My job as SIM representative involved the daily work of processing mail, typing letters, general administration, recruiting candidates, promoting SIM, nurturing prayer groups, distributing literature and the like. It wasn't my cup of tea at all. I longed to be back in Benin among the Boko people working on the Boko Bible and all the varied ministries that I did out there. In Australia I also had to preach in church services, conduct home meetings, show films and help missionaries who came home from overseas for a break. Sometimes I had to travel to country areas, sometimes interstate.

Our return to Benin was delayed again by one year when we found that Joy was expecting our fourth child.

In December Dad entered St Vincent's Hospital for a bowel-cancer operation and he returned in January for further surgery. The doctors told him he would have to abstain from alcohol and over the following months he felt better than he had for years.

On February 2nd, 1979 Peter Ross was born at St George's hospital in Kew. Joy enjoyed having a baby in an Australian hospital for the first time with all the attention they gave.

In June we met with our church leaders and our mission director and it was decided that we should not return to Benin at this time.

Joy suffered occasionally from asthma and bronchitis and was still emotionally fragile. And now she had four boys under eight to care for. She was having counselling sessions, and reluctantly I joined them. The pressure was adversely affecting our marriage. This was my dark night of the soul. Where had I gone wrong? It seemed that I had been so enthusiastic about my ministry that I had neglected my wife. Joy wasn't feeling like going back to Africa again.

Later that year, after attending a football match with Joy where we were subjected to a lot of bad language by surrounding supporters, I wrote a letter to the editor of the Age newspaper. I was complaining about the drop in moral standards that we had seen in Australia on an increasing basis since the 1960s. The letter was published under the title; "We're a nation of blasphemers." It went like this: I said that blasphemy, more than anything else, is a repudiation of God and an insult to his holy person. It is also an insult to all who honor the name of God and his Son, Jesus Christ. In Africa the name of God is honored, and common greetings are: 'God bless you!', 'God save us!', or 'God wake us up well!' In Australia by contrast the name of God is usually spoken idly in surprise, anger or as an oath, e.g. 'Good God!', 'By God!', 'Lord above!', 'Jesus Christ!', 'Jesus!', 'Geez!', 'Gee!'. You can't go to the football or a public place without hearing a barrage of such blasphemy. Australians cannot sink lower than this in their speech. It may show utter contempt for God. The least it shows is that there is no personal relationship between God and the blasphemer. The great Australian adjective "bloody" also comes into the category of blasphemy. Why is a word derived from blood so popular? People obviously don't know why they use it. Suffice that it is 'smart' and shows that a person has arrived at 'maturity'. The whole basis of Christian salvation is the blood of Jesus Christ shed on the cross at Calvary. That is why the word 'bloody' is blasphemous, and that is why it is so popular.

Blasphemy is so common and so unreasonable; it is beyond human explanation. Satan the father of lies who deceives the whole world is blinding people so that they cannot see the relevance of the Christian gospel. The Third Commandment states: "You shall not misuse the name of the Lord your God, for the Lord will not hold anyone guiltless, who misuses his name." Jesus said: "By your words you will be acquitted, and by your words you will be condemned." So, beware.

Age journalist Iola Matthews followed up my letter with an article entitled: "By Heck! We're such a foul-mouthed mob," in which she said: "Missionary Mr. Ross Jones is right. Not only are we a profane lot, but lurid language is rapidly becoming publicly acceptable." Unfortunately, the trend has continued.

In September 1979 we moved up to Sydney to work in the SIM national office. Joy spent each Thursday at the office as Australian editor of the SIM bimonthly magazine Africa Now. I was Publications Secretary and assistant to the Australian Director with administrative duties, including the processing of missionary candidates.

Within a week of arriving in Sydney we bought a house in Cronulla, sixteen miles from the office, but only a five-minute walk from the Cronulla surf beach, of which I made good use. Buying this house was an inspiration of Joy's father. We bought it for $66,000 from a Christian agent who was a friend of Neville's and with the financial help of several relatives. We moved in two days later and Andrew continued his schooling at Woolooware Primary.

In 1980 Andrew and Paul both attended the local school while Joy and I did our jobs at the national office. In March I contacted thirty-five churches in the Sutherland Shire where we lived. I was looking for meetings to promote the work of SIM, and half of the churches responded, so I was busy speaking in Sunday services morning and evening for the next few months.

Dad and Flo paid us a visit in April. He had told us in a letter that he had found a new friend, Jesus, who had made a great difference to his life. That was unbelievably great news for us. He was a great gardener, and one day he pruned his roses and put the clippings in the boot of his car to take them to the local tip. While there, he noticed a new book that had been thrown out. When he picked it up, he saw that it was a Bible. He took it home saying to himself: "If anyone else had seen this Bible, surely they would have taken it. God must have meant it for me." This sparked faith in his heart and from that day until he died, he was a new person. Even my sister, who is not a Christian, recognized that he had found God, and that there was a great difference in his life. We were so happy to see that my father had found faith in Jesus. Every time we had visited him at Maffra, we had tried to talk to him about the Lord. Sometimes he would listen, but not for long. One day Joy was challenging him, and he said: "That's enough." Joy said: "No, I haven't finished what I want to say yet." Then Dad said: "I'm being attacked in my own house!" Now finally at the age of seventy-seven, having been off the 'grog' for a year, he put his faith in the Savior whom he had learnt so much about in his youth.

In May we had a talk with the acting director of SIM Australia and it was decided that we would return to Benin in November. Joy said that having had this extended break in Australia, she was ready to go back to Benin for one more four-year term, so that the Boko New Testament could be published. Of course, I was very much relieved and excited at the prospect of getting back into my work in Africa.

We would no longer be living at isolated Bobena. We would live at Segbana where there was a vacant mission home, with a Post Office over the road and a petrol station not far away. Andrew and Paul, who were eight and six respectively, would attend Kent Academy boarding school at Miango in Nigeria.

We thought that when we finally returned from Africa we would like to settle in Melbourne, so I enquired about selling the Cronulla house. Our neighbor agreed to sell our properties together and we sold our house for $98,000, a profit of $32,000 in one year! I looked in the Melbourne Age for suitable homes and we went to Melbourne with several in mind. The first house we looked at was a four-bedroom two-bathroom home in Glen Waverley. It was a palace compared to what we were used to, and it won our hearts. We bought it at auction and paid $75,000 cash. God is so good. Joy knew she had a nice home to come home to, and this gave her courage as we ventured forth again to West Africa.

Ministry at Segbana

1981-1984

Boko Bible school graduates

We left Melbourne on November 25th 1980, and flew to Cotonou via Rome and Lagos. It was always an adventure flying half way around the world with four young boys in tow, but they were always good and cooperative. We all had attacks of diarrhea as we settled into Segbana and adjusted to different water and bugs.

Having been away from the Boko work for three years, it was encouraging to see the growing spiritual maturity of the church leaders and the progress of the Boko church in general. Before Christmas a two-day conference was held at Bobena with seventy in attendance. It was completely organized and conducted by the Bible school students, some of whom were acting pastors in their villages. They preached well and discussed problems encountered in the five Boko churches. At Bobena in our absence, the numbers in the church had dropped from seventy to fifteen. No doubt some only attended in the past because we lived there, but a serious rift occurred when the pastor took a strong stand against female circumcision (clitoridectomy), a cruel practice where the clitoris of young girls is cut out with a sharp knife at the local shea butter processing place. The older women have much authority and are sure that girls won't have safe delivery of babies if their clitoris is intact. In fact, the opposite was true as a result of scaring. As a result of this stand, which had to be taken by the Christians sooner or later, women had fallen away from the church, and also young men who had been told they wouldn't be given wives, if they were going to refuse to circumcise their daughters.

In mid-January we drove to Gurai where Joy said sad goodbyes to Andrew and Paul. I accompanied them on their flight to Miango to help them settle in to boarding school. On my return I brought home one-hundred chicks in an effort to improve the stock of the Boko chickens.

In March, Joy and I drove to Miango for a short holiday to see how the boys were coping with their new lifestyle. Near the Niger/Nigeria border the gear stick snapped off at the floor and we had to travel in second gear for an hour or so before getting it welded back on. Andrew had made new friends and was rising to the challenge of the American curriculum. Paul had his difficulties settling in, being timid, and confused by the American accents. Andrew and Paul already had American accents themselves.

Back at Segbana, we bought a small generator, which we found had some parts missing, but four months later we had it working. For the first time we had fluorescent lights which were so much brighter than kerosene lamps, and a fan which gave much relief in the hot season.

As well as her daily medical work at the dispensary Joy began a women's meeting on Tuesday mornings where they had craft, Bible stories, and Scripture memorization. I had a Tuesday night Bible study with the men. One Sunday I preached at Lugu on the text: "It is better for you to enter the kingdom of God with one eye than to have two eyes and be be thrown into hell" (Mark 9:47). There was a blind man at church that day for the first time, having just made his decision to follow Jesus. Three weeks later he died.

In June Andrew and Paul came home for three months holiday. It was great to have them with us and Matthew and Peter once again. They had a bicycle to ride, a monkey named 'Chiko', and a dog named 'Fella'. My chickens started dying and after consulting books I found that they were loaded with ticks causing paralysis. Then Joy came down with hepatitis! She was in bed for three weeks with nausea and aches and a poor appetite. We didn't go out to see a doctor for a month because Joy wasn't up to the three-hour bumpy road trip.

A Canadian government aid program helped SIM linguists get better equipped. This enabled us to obtain a new duplicating machine and typewriter and even a new Peugeot 504 station wagon. We translated and printed ten booklets that year: Mark's gospel, Parables of Jesus, "It's true, everyone should know", which was in cartoon form (Scripture Union), Heart of Man, Jesus Story 1 & 2, Animal fables, Basic health book, Genesis, and the Story of Joseph.

We had a lot more visitors than in the past, including some Aussie missionaries working in neighboring countries. We also had regular visits by African preachers who came to teach and encourage the Boko Christians. With Islam the dominant religion it was important for them to know that there were many more Christians around, both in Benin and other countries.

After happy times of family togetherness Andrew and Paul returned to school. When their plane was refused permission to fly, they spent eight hours travelling in a taxi truck, arriving at Miango in the early hours of the morning.

In September I started the revision of the New Testament with three helpers: Levi, André, and Moses. From time to time we had a regional consultant from the United Bible Society come and check our work. He was a bit dogmatic and did not accept other people's ideas. I had a few altercations with him and to this day I believe I was right.

Our boys were to come home at Christmas and their passports were sent to Lagos to get new visas. The passports were returned to Jos, but then a taxi driver stole the briefcase they were in from a missionary. People prayed, and one evening someone walked into the mission hospital with the briefcase and passports. The money had been removed and the briefcase thrown into a gutter nearby.

On December 19th three missionary families were eagerly awaiting the small plane bringing their children home for Christmas. We were at a remote airstrip near Gaya in Niger Republic, when all of a sudden, a government official drove up and declared the airstrip closed as he rolled 55-gallon drums onto the runway. The plane was already due to land. Two of the dads went with the official to see a superior, while the mums and I had a time of prayer on the runway. When the superior learned that our children were coming home for Christmas, he relented, and we rolled the drums off the runway. Just then the plane appeared and landed, emptying its precious cargo. We praised God for these seeming miracles. But after Christmas, when these same children had to return to the school from the same airstrip, permission was not granted, and the drums remained on the runway. The plane came and circled for two hours before returning to Niamey. Negotiations continued for six hours and finally the children were put in one family's car and driven to Niamey to meet the plane and fly back to school the following day.

February 5th, 1982 was our tenth wedding anniversary. We thanked God for happiness and for each other. A SIM missionary visited us and using Child Evangelism methods taught fourteen Boko how to start Sunday schools in their churches, and how Christian parents should bring up their children. As a result, four Sunday Schools were started with up to forty children in each one.

Boko Christians stick out like sore thumbs in Boko society. Although they are a small minority, everyone knows about them. They only have one wife, they don't give their children away to relatives to bring up, they don't sacrifice to the spirits or get involved in black magic, and they don't have their daughters circumcised. They aren't admired for this, but at least the non-Christians know that Christians are prepared to be different, to do what they feel is right because of their faith, even in the face of persecution. It was often remarked that the Christians always look so healthy.

Around this time Joy wrote the following about a busy day she had had:

> There they were, before eight a.m., a small crowd of sick and injured, all waiting for treatment. Measles, the great child-killer of West Africa, had recently come to town, so the number of sick children had increased. At 9 a.m. Ross left for two days of Bible School at Bobena. At 11 a.m. Matthew's correspondence lessons for the day were begun but were interrupted soon after by Paul's screams. A child had thrown a metal dart into his leg. Then there was lunch to prepare and serve to four hungry boys. After lunch all was quiet for about an hour until Paul became aware that he couldn't bend his knee or walk well. Peter awoke from his sleep and needed some mothering. Matthew' lessons had to be completed. There was tea to prepare, baths to be run, bedtime stories to be read, and finally prayers with each one.

Sometimes life is a hassle. Very busy days produce tensions. Emotions are continually tried to their limits. Depression tends to rear its ugly head with its crippling symptoms: sluggishness, headache, chronic fatigue, loss of self-esteem and indecision.

Meanwhile the translation team had revised up to the book of Romans, two new men had joined Bible school, and sixteen people at Serebani had given their names to Boko evangelists and said that they wanted to become Christians. My right-hand man, Levi, recorded six half-hour programs in Boko, based on Genesis 1-11. They began and ended with Boko hymn singing and were aired over a government radio station in Ilorin, Nigeria once a month.

In December 1982, accompanied by four church leaders, I visited ten Boko villages in Nigeria. After formalities with customs, police and the local chief, we drove down a track to Deaagbezi, a village where Levi's aunt lived. After the evening meal, David began singing with the children and soon one-hundred people of all ages came to listen. Levi preached using a picture chart. Several people asked questions. The next day we preached in five villages and left cassette players and tapes with them. We were burdened for this un-evangelized area of Nigeria, but we didn't have the personnel or time to cope with all the opportunities. Nearly thirty-five years later the Boko people there are still largely unreached, but there are some African missionaries working in the area.

Dad's Passing

---◆---

1983

Dad and my step-mother Flo (1968)

We heard that my Dad's health was deteriorating. His cancer had spread to his lungs, and we made a quick decision to go home for Christmas and spend some time with him while he was still alive, rather than going home for his funeral.

Our first stop was the mission HQ at Parakou, where we stayed at the Guest House. We were in a unit near the back wall of the property, three of us in one room and the three older boys in the other. At 4:45 a.m. we awoke to hear some men running past our door, followed by the night guard calling out "Thief! Thief!" The thieves scaled the wall near our room and disappeared into the darkness. I went out to see if the guard was alright, and he asked me to come and see where the thieves had been. They had tried to get into a big safe in the business department. Nothing was taken as the guard had disturbed them. While I was talking to the guard, I heard what sounded like a goat's cries. Then I realized it was Joy screaming for help. I was a great sprinter under such circumstances.

I had left Joy and the boys back in the room. A short time after I had gone, Joy heard a shuffling noise outside the door. She asked who was there but received no reply. Suddenly two tall men dressed totally in black and armed with knives came into the room. One shut the door, while the other walked towards Joy with knife outstretched. The one at the door grabbed my trousers and leather jacket and stuffed them into a bag. Joy of course was terrified and stood up and started screaming like mad. The men became unnerved and quickly left, and a little later I arrived and asked what had happened. I locked the door and tried to calm Joy who said she wouldn't spend another night in that place. As for the boys, they slept through it all.

At daybreak I ventured out and climbed over the wall to see if I could find my clothing. Unfortunately for the thieves there wasn't a brass razoo in my pockets, but my car keys were. I saw some blood on top of the wall where a thief had injured himself, and then I found my clothes thrown away by the side of the road, with keys intact.

We travelled on to Cotonou that day. Then we received some awful news which made our hearts sink. Two nights later the thieves had returned. They killed the guard, cut off his ears, removed the safe from the wall, and stole $600. It was the guard's ears that caused him to disturb them the night we were there. That is why they cut them off.

We arrived home just in time to spend Christmas with Dad and Stu and Libs at Maffra. A week later we went to Sydney to spend several weeks with Joy's parents. Then we lived in Chadstone for two months, at the Uniting Church missionary homes. The older boys attended Bayview Primary and Peter started kindergarten. We visited people and were visited. Joy spoke at the women's convention in Bright and we enjoyed fellowship at our church in Murrumbeena. Every second or third weekend we went to Maffra to visit Dad who was in and out of hospital. It was sad to see his deteriorating physical condition but comforting to know that he was trusting in Jesus. We spent Easter with him and said our final farewell, and then we travelled to Sydney to spend our last week with Joy's parents.

We had a hassled trip back to Benin with hotel problems in Rome, then I lost my camera, and we had an unwanted overnight stay at Abidjan airport.

On arrival back at Segbana we found the house safe, but filthy. Our water drum had rusted through, so there was no water in the house for five days, and our houseboy had fallen into immorality. We found a new one, but he had to go to Nigeria for a month. The temperature was 38° every day with hot nights to match. Joy had stomach problems for several weeks, Pete had a bout of bacillary dysentery, and then Matthew fell out of a mango tree and chipped his elbow. Then we had an accident on our way to Parakou. Heavy rain had made a deep, wide gully across the road. We came around a bend and there it was. There was no chance of stopping in time, and we hit the far side of the gaping hole bending a front wheel against the body and putting a hole in the radiator. I was stuck in the African bush with Joy and our two younger boys. No mobile phones in those days, but we were on a main road. After a short time, a German volunteer worker arrived and towed us forty miles to Kandi. We took the Land Rover to some backyard mechanics. They welded the radiator and chained the vehicle to a tree and pushed it back and forth until the wheel straightened up. $60! Someone suggested that we get the alignment checked when we arrived in Parakou. It seemed to travel well, and at Parakou the mechanics said that the alignment was spot-on. My favorite verse in these situations was Psalm 34:19 "The righteous person may have many troubles, but the Lord delivers him from them all."

On July 15th we received news from Australia via telegram and government radio that Dad had passed into the presence of the Lord. I was expecting this news and wasn't too sad. I was thankful that we had gone home to see him. The message I received said; "Come down immediately." I was more confused by this statement than I was by Dad's death. Later when we went to Parakou, we discovered that these words weren't on the original telegram. An over-zealous African added the words thinking that they had been omitted.

Printing the Boko New Testament

1984

The Boko New Testament

One morning a young Christian came to my office with a question. "A friend is making counterfeit notes but can't get the watermark right. Can you help him?" It seemed too incredible to be true. I dismissed the question and told him to have no part in criminal activities and to not have such friends.

Two months later when passing the police station, I saw him with a friend, standing there with long faces. The friend had been caught passing counterfeit notes in a Boko village. When the police grilled my friend, he said that he had told me about it several months back and that I had warned him not to have anything to do with it. Then the police summoned me to the police station and asked me what I knew. Why hadn't I reported the matter to them when I first heard about it? I told them I couldn't believe it was real. Later the main culprits escaped prison, probably having bribed their way out, and my friend was put in prison for a year. When we went to Nigeria to see our boys, the rumor was spread among the Boko that I was involved in forgery and had fled the country.

Amos' fiancée Rachel lived in Segbana and wanted to go to Kandi to learn French and sewing. Some missionaries there were happy to look after her. Her family was Muslim, and she was being persecuted for her faith in Jesus and for her desire to marry a Christian. Her father told her to leave home if that is what she wanted. The Segbana church leaders discussed her case and decided that she should go with me to Kandi the following week, as I was making a trip to Parakou. They told her to tell her family where she was going, but she was afraid and didn't do it. After I left for Kandi, her family was furious and retaliated by going to the police. The police then arrested Levi, the President of the Boko church and my main translation helper. He was to be put in prison until she was brought back, because it was he who had called her to come when I was leaving.

When returning from Parakou, I was met on the road by a messenger who told me Levi was in prison and I had to bring Rachel back. I returned to Kandi, collected Rachel and arrived in Segbana late that night. She and Levi had to sleep at the police station that night but were released the next morning.

The court met to discuss the matter. The father said he did not want his daughter to be a Christian or to marry a Christian. The police said the law of the land decreed that everyone was free to choose their own religion and the person they married. The father's effort to cause trouble for the Christians was thwarted, and Rachel later went to Kandi.

In September the boys went back to Kent Academy, and Matthew went with them for the first time. In October the revision of the New Testament was completed. Not many verses had remained the same. Our manuscripts were sent to a neighboring country Togo to be keyed into the computer there and the printouts were sent back to us for a final reading. While reading the printouts we discovered some complicated grammatical rules concerning Boko pronouns. These were logophoric pronouns! This resulted in changing the tone on half the pronouns in the New Testament. Back went our corrections to our frustrated typesetters. Boko has three basic pronouns, high, mid and low, but noun phrases and pronouns never end in a low tone. They end in a semilow tone which is halfway between low and mid. I was working in Boko for twenty-six years before I discovered that!

Helen Johnstone, whom I knew from Bible school, and who worked for Gospel Recordings came and put Matthew and Revelation on cassette for us, narrated by some good Boko readers.

When we went to Miango to visit our boys, Andrew was on crutches and Matthew was sick with a virus. Andrew's Nigerian friend had pulled him down from a cupboard and he had broken his leg. We had three happy weeks with them and learnt that Matthew had settled in well.

After Christmas the whole family went camping by a river in the bush for a few days. Levi and I went hunting on New Year's Eve for cane rats but ending up with a python. Levi saw it in the long grass, but his gun wouldn't fire. He called me over with my .22 rifle and I stood over it and fired two pellets into its head. I put the dead snake around my neck and dragged it back to the camp where it was roasted.

We heard on the radio that there was a military coup in Nigeria and wondered if our boys would get back to school on time. After some hassles with local government authorities they flew off in a SIMair plane one day late. The plane however was not allowed to go further than Kano and they travelled the last leg by bus. SIM let us know by radio that they had arrived safely.

In late March we went to Miango for our holiday and enjoyed four weeks with the boys. We were packed and ready to leave next morning when we heard on the radio that all the borders were closed for twelve days while Nigeria changed its currency. After three-and-a-half weeks we were allowed to leave Nigeria by air. From Cotonou we took the train to Parakou, and then we travelled by road back to Segbana.

The Boko New Testament was to be typeset by Wycliffe Bible Translators at their base in Dallas, Texas. Cheap excursion fares by KLM helped us to decide that we would all go and make it a family experience. We travelled 440 miles by road to Lomé in Togo, then we flew to Amsterdam and Houston in Texas, and then on to Dallas where we had our own apartment. The boys (and me!) enjoyed a day at Wet n Wild Fun Park with its wonderful water slides. The apartment block had its own swimming pool and the boys learnt to swim there. I found that the easiest way to teach them to swim was to throw them in at the deep end and then be ready to throw them a floater, or to jump in and help them myself.

On the first day the typesetter did a verse check and told me very bluntly that the manuscript was not in good enough shape for typesetting, because there were verses missing. This infuriated me because I had spent so much time making sure everything was shipshape. He hadn't taken into consideration the fact that the numbering of verses in the French Bible, which we followed, was different to the English. After that things went smoothly.

The typesetting took seven weeks, but Joy and the boys had to return to Benin without me a week earlier than that, because their excursion tickets were expiring. The typeset manuscript was sent to a printer in England and from there it was to be air-freighted to Benin before we left for Australia.

Back at Segbana, the translation team resumed the translation of Psalms and Proverbs. Our three boys flew off for their final term at Kent Academy. The borders had been closed for five months and the Nigerian government gave special permission for them to return in a mission plane.

We had planned to have the New Testaments arrive at Segbana well before we left, so that we could dedicate them at the annual Boko Church conference in December, and to see the Christian's joy, but they didn't arrive in time. A paper shortage and then problems with the color illustrations caused delays. We saw one copy in Cotonou the day before we left Benin and were able to show it to one Boko Christian.

Late afternoon on January 3rd many Christians came from their villages to honor us with a farewell feast, a sad and moving occasion. They served pork, rice, and African soup and expressed their thanks to us for our service among them. Next morning, we were up early, breakfasted and packed ready to leave. Many people came and stood around as we did this. The car was crammed with our luggage, our four kids and the dog and we drove off as the pastors and Christians sang one of our favorite Boko choruses. All this was rather heart-rending as we left behind many loved friends.

The next day we said goodbye to our missionary co-workers at Parakou. Over the years many of them had become like family to us and we enjoyed working with them on the SIM Benin team. For Joy it was her last goodbye to the Boko people. I expected to come back, but I wasn't sure how things would work out.

THE BOKO BIBLE AND JOY'S ARTHRITIS

1985-1991

Dedication of the Boko Bible at Segbana

In January 1985 we moved into our home at 12 Crown Street, Glen Waverley, the home we had bought four years previously. The rent we collected during those years was used to furnish the home. I went to Young's Auctions in Camberwell and bought beds, lounge, dining room setting and all that was needed. It was second-hand, but good quality. I bought my first computer; a Sharp PC 5000 with a built-in printer. It used heat sensitive paper and there were only eight lines on the screen. But it was a computer! The difference a computer makes for a Bible translator is amazing. From now on, whenever I wanted to revise a verse or chapter or even a book, I just had to key in the corrections rather than typing up the whole manuscript again. With the help of programs from Wycliffe, I began keying in all the Old Testament books that we had translated into Boko.

Here I was back in Australia to live. That was a disappointment, my heart was in Benin. I knew that the boys needed to come home and integrate into Australian society before their secondary school years got too advanced, but that could have waited a couple of years more. But then again, I knew that life in Africa wasn't easy for Joy and she had already made a heroic effort, so I didn't complain. I planned to give the Boko church at least half the Old Testament and had requested that I continue to work on it at Glen Waverley for the next two years with trips back to Benin as necessary. So, I still had hope.

Meanwhile the boys all started their new schools in Melbourne. Andrew started year seven at Scotch College at Hawthorn. We had bought a house in Glen Waverley because Scotch was next to Kooyong station which was on the Glen Waverley line. Because I was an old boy and we were in Christian ministry we were able to send the boys to Scotch at one-third fees. This was a tremendous help as private school fees are expensive, and for four years, we had three boys attending there at the same time. Andrew had a slight American accent, a vestige of the boarding school in Nigeria. A fellow student said to him: "I hate Americans." Andrew gently protested: "I'm not American." "I hate you anyway," was the caustic reply. After coming from a sheltered Christian school, this was a rude awakening to Aussie banter.

Paul, Matthew and Peter all attended Syndal Primary which was very close to our home; they could easily walk to and from school. They didn't have too much trouble fitting into Australian schools, but the bad language was a new phenomenon they had to get used to.

In addition to looking after the boys and domestic duties Joy led a monthly SIM prayer meeting and a weekly Bible study at Murrumbeena church. Her parents lived up in Sydney, but Neville came down and stayed with us for two weeks in March and his wife, Bessie, came for ten days in April. We were missionary guests at the Wimmera Easter Convention at Warracknabeal and enjoyed telling people about our work among the Boko. There were meetings to speak at every month throughout that year and the years following.

Then in July, Joy developed rheumatoid arthritis in her hands and feet.

Letters from Benin told of delays in getting the New Testaments. Two hundred copies had been received, but they sold out immediately. We always had problems getting the Scriptures into the hands of the people, more problems than what seemed 'normal'.

In September I returned to Benin for twelve weeks. After flying 18,000 miles which was the easy part, I had a train trip to Parakou. The engine broke down and we had to wait for another engine to come. Then it took eight hours by road to do the last two-hundred miles. We checked books that I had worked on during the year and then translated Isaiah, Joel, Jonah, Malachi and Ecclesiastes. I borrowed a generator to charge my computer in the evenings, but after three nights it blew up. The Muslim owners wanted me to pay them $500. A government official got involved and eventually I paid $135. After that the official let me charge my computer at his house until the local prison was opened. The mission house was then connected to the prison generator and I had power for the rest of my stay.

The Boko literacy committee elected me as honorary president, a pleasant vote of confidence from the non-Christian community. They requested that I produce a Boko grammar and dictionary, something I had always wanted to do. There were baptisms in three villages while I was there, including Bobena where the church had halved in numbers, but was now thriving again.

Fifteen young men spent ten days at Segbana making 1,800 cement blocks for the Christian bookshop which I was financing with gifts from supporters. The foundations had been dug and the shop was to be run by the SIM related UEEB church, Union of Evangelical Churches of Benin. They ran two other bookshops in Benin. Every two weeks I spent two days at the Bible School at Bobena, which met in our old home, teaching twelve pastors and evangelists. In addition, Levi and I travelled six-hundred miles on motor-bike visiting Boko churches and some new areas.

While I was in Benin, Joy's father lived at our home and was a great help. But Joy's hands and feet deteriorated tremendously, and she started seeing a specialist. She was put on medication which stabilized the condition somewhat. This was the beginning of what would prove to be a very painful journey.

In March 1986 we had a healing service for Joy in our home with our pastor and deacons. She started teaching Religious Education in a primary school the same month. In July, Andrew was returning from an overnight hike in the Tallarook forest with other Scotch boys, when the edge of the road gave away, and the bus rolled over and down a mountain. Miraculously no boys were seriously hurt. In September Andrew rededicated his life to the Lord at a Bill Newman crusade, and he had the joy of seeing a schoolmate coming to know the Lord.

In September, I returned to Benin again on what was to be my last trip to Africa. The translation team daily sensed the prayers of God's people as we constantly covered more ground than anticipated. During the first month at Segbana, we checked work I had done during the year, verse by verse. In the second month we translated more of the prophetical books. Levi always worked tirelessly. His wife, Mary, and their four children lived on the mission property. Thorough checking and proofreading remained before this work would be ready for publication.

It was great to meet a Swiss/German couple, Robert and Cornelia Hablutzel who had arrived in Segbana in February. They were immersed in Boko language study and planned to do pastor training. The bookshop cum reading room was completed and six tables and twenty-four chairs made. When leaving for Australia, I gave my dedicated co-worker Levi a treat; I took him down to Cotonou. We flew in a Fokker Friendship from Parakou, and when we arrived at Cotonou, I showed him the sea. We had translated the word often, but he had never seen it before.

Jesus said: "And I tell you that you are Peter, and on this rock I will build my church, and the gates of Hades will not overcome it" (Matthew 16:18). It was exciting to see the Boko church developing so well in their Muslim society. Early every morning while I was at Segbana there was a prayer meeting which went for an hour. There were never less than ten men there and this was the practice in all seven of the Boko churches. Another thing that impressed me was the singing. Three churches had formed choirs of young people, and at Segbana they had seven instruments, including a piano accordion that used to belong to Bryan Greenwood. They are always composing new choruses and they sing with enthusiasm and clapping, and later when it was authorized, body movement. Africans are very musical and they love to put their whole body and soul into it.

Robert Hablutzel started teaching at Bible School and he had eight new men starting, making a total of twenty. Three of the students had moved with their families to other villages to start new churches, and one pastor already had thirty-six followers. They are not paid a salary, the churches are too poor, so they spend half their time farming.

On my way home in the plane I was correcting manuscripts of the Minor Prophets that we had just translated. When I got off the plane at Sydney for a short break, an enthusiastic cleaner took the papers out of the pocket of my seat. When I returned and discovered the papers missing, I was in a fluster, but was told: "It will have already been shredded. Sorry!" My heart sank. We had so enjoyed translating those books and now there wouldn't be another chance. But wait, there was a duplicate copy at Segbana. When I reached home, I phoned, and the Hablutzels soon had it in the post for me.

In February 1987 we celebrated our fifteenth wedding anniversary and praised God for our marriage and its many blessings. Joy began weekly gold injections for the arthritis as the previous treatment wasn't halting progress of the disease. All her joints were now giving her trouble from time to time.

I photocopied all the Boko Old Testament manuscripts and posted four copies off to Benin for final checking. My two years was up with the work still not completed, so I requested another year, and the International Bible Society was contacted concerning publication. News from Segbana was encouraging. Six more villages were building churches and new groups were forming in other places. The church was spreading right throughout the Boko area.

Andrew at fourteen was growing, and up to my eyes, and he was having a good year. He took part in coffee shop evangelism at Wonthaggi, where he had good talks with needy teenagers. Then we went together on a three-day hike through Wilson's Promontory with young people from our church. Later he went to Passage Island in Bass Strait with a friend from school. We all went to the Foundation Day concert to see him playing the timpani in the school orchestra. Andrew, Paul and Matthew all took part in the World Vision forty-hour famine, while Peter, not to be outdone, went in the 'Food busters' for smaller children.

The boys were good. Joy was a good mother showing interest in everything they did and praying with them every night before they went to bed. We were disciplinarians to a certain extent. The boys all had domestic duties, especially as Joy's body broke down. Every night after dinner we had devotions and prayed together, and they were expected to exhibit Christian character.

Joy's arthritis regressed a lot in mid-year. Her shoulders were now troublesome, and the gold injections caused mouth ulcers. Three cortisone injections in joints and an innersole for her right shoe brought some relief. All this didn't stop her from speaking to fifty-five women at a Chinese restaurant in July.

In October we organized the buying of an apartment for Joy's parents just around the corner from where we lived. They moved down from Sydney in December. Joy was an only child, and our boys were their only grandchildren, so it was wonderful that they could be so close to us.

All the boys did well at school. Andrew was baptized at Murrumbeena in December, while Paul was presented with six badges at Boy's Brigade for various activities. He also did well at cross country running and in the 800 meters.

I joined the Evangelical Alliance Evangelism Department committee and was responsible for doing a survey of Victorian churches, with the aim of finding what areas of the State lacked evangelical witness. I divided the State into 210 areas and looked for a contact person in each area to distribute questionnaires. When the survey was finished, it gave us a good indication of the percentage of churchgoers in each area and the main characteristics of each church.

66 percent of the Old Testament had been completed and consultant checking was being done by SIL Bible consultants at their base in Kangaroo Ground. SIM leaders were negotiating with the International Bible Society as to whether I should complete the Boko Bible. We were happy when I was given the go-ahead to finish the Boko Bible in the next few years. The main concern was that it be adequately checked, firstly by my workers in Benin, and secondly by translation consultants who are sometimes hard to come by.

In 1988 Joy's Ladies Bible study group grew from five to thirteen. This group went for many years and was a great blessing to many people. I was a deacon at Murrumbeena Baptist Church and the boys were involved in youth groups, so there was a lot of driving back and forth to Murrumbeena. We bought bunks for Matthew and Peter and within a week they both fell off the top bunk, Matthew breaking both bones in his lower right arm. The angle of his arm was a sickening sight. We were thankful that there was a doctor living next door. Paul was doing well with his trumpet lessons and he made his first public appearance at a young people's service.

I made another successful trip to Benin in July-August 1988. We revised seven books and translated four new ones. We found better expressions for covenant, kingdom of God, tabernacle, brimstone, incense, grace, offering, feast, tithe, censer, chewing the cud, and peace. There was a lot of work in making corrections to every occurrence of these words in the earlier books that we had done, including the New Testament. On Sundays Levi and I visited the churches on motorbike. Being the wet season, we got caught in the rain a couple of times and had to cross a couple of swollen creeks, but it was great seeing the new churches in worship; men on one side of the aisle, women on the other, and the musicians up front. There were now thirteen Boko villages with churches in Benin and nine in Nigeria.

Meanwhile back at home Joy had cortisone injections in a troublesome knee and hand, but she was able to continue her Bible class and RE ministries. As usual she did a great job holding the fort while I was away, despite her handicap, and the boys pulled their weight as well.

At the beginning of 1989 Joy said:

> In recent months I again have asked the Lord concerning my arthritis, and now I have come to some conclusions. I believe that through some of life's more trying experiences, God works out his perfect will in a life, giving that life a character that is more usable and very much able to sympathize with others who face similar experiences. Our minister preached on John 9, the healing of the man born blind, and verse three spoke to me. This happened, "that the works of God might be displayed in him."

Andrew went to Queenscliff beach mission for thirteen days. It said it was great fun, and he learnt a lot about kids and how to minister to them. It was sad when they had to depart. The mission had been a success and many good friends had been made. He came home praising the Lord for all he had done and the great time it had been. He hopes to go again at the end of this year.

During the September holidays our family went to Expo '88. It was a lot of fun as there was so much to see and do. In January I took the four boys on a camp; we spent four days travelling through the forests of Victoria. We slept three nights at different campsites: Toorongo Falls near Noojee, Mt Matlock and Walhalla. Matthew and Paul did some fishing, but it was unsuccessful, because Peter's method of catching fish was to throw rocks at them.

Matthew was learning clarinet for a year and doing quite well. He did his grade three exams and was soon to begin secondary school at Scotch College. He said he wanted to find good friends at school and be able to witness to them about what Jesus meant to him.

As for Pete, he was ten and started tennis lessons. His aim in life was to be like Andre Agassi!

That gives you an idea as to how our boys were developing.

In October 1989 I went to Benin and worked with the translation team on the eight books that we translated that year. I had a good team of four experienced, mature men. As usual we made lots of changes as the translation becomes more idiomatic. On December 6th the translation of the Boko Bible was completed, but, a year of final checking by myself in Australia and the team at Segbana was to follow. Levi is a tireless worker. He teaches regularly at the Bible School at Bobena, he teaches the young men on Wednesday nights at Segbana, on Sundays he travels to check up on all the Boko churches, and morning and evening he is hard at work with the Bible translation.

I witnessed nine baptisms at Bobena in November and in the new year there were thirty-one more; forty people altogether from seven different villages. Two new churches were built at Monrou and Nasikonzi. Although there were now fifteen Boko churches in Benin, the work in Nigeria was slow. One of our pastors there died of a strangulated hernia. A Nigerian missionary there was attacked on the road. The robbers took $150 and his motorbike, and broke eight of his teeth.

In December 1989 the Benin government announced that they were changing course; Marxism/Leninism was now history for Benin.

Andrew was progressing well. At seventeen he started teaching Sunday School and was a member of the church youth Council. He was dux in Geography in year eleven and then went on beach mission in January. Paul did well in diving and went to New Zealand to play trumpet with the school orchestra. Matthew was enjoying playing his clarinet and was learning Russian at school and did well at swimming backstroke. Pete was still at primary school and doing well in cross country runs. In the first match of the cricket season Peter was bowling the last over of the day against Jordanville. Three balls to go ... three batsmen out!

Joy was having a difficult time with her knees at this time and her hands and feet continued to get crippled. She started a new treatment, but the medications could not cure, they could only slow the progress and relieve the pain.

Throughout 1990 Levi, Gabriel, and André did a verse by verse check of every Old Testament book and sent me the books by post month by month. I evaluated their suggestions and corrected the master copy. The job was long and tedious. The Bible is the Word of God; we didn't want there to be any mistakes.

Here are some examples of corrections we made. The 'fattened calf' had been translated as 'fatty calf'; we changed it to one that had put on weight. The expression 'Kingdom of God' was changed from 'God's kingdom' to 'kingdom from God', because it doesn't refer to God's universal reign, but to the coming Messianic kingdom of which Jesus is the King. 'Unleavened bread' was translated as 'bread without leaven', but in Boko if bread hasn't risen it is not bread, it is cake. The word 'righteous' had been translated by an adjective meaning 'straight, upright, correct'. I was shocked and incredulous when the team told me that this would only be interpreted as somebody who stood straight and erect. We settled for 'good'. The righteous are good people, not erect ones.

Andrew was doing his final year of high school and wasn't helped by an attack of appendicitis in July. His ruptured appendix was removed immediately at the Monash Medical Centre.

Murrumbeena Baptist had been asked by the Baptist Union if they could revive the church at Ormond which had stopped meeting. Being involved in church planting in Benin I was appointed to coordinate that endeavor. We did a lot of advertising and the opening service was on October 28th, 1990 with 113 in attendance. Later attendance averaged sixty-four. The new church was initially called Caulfield Baptist, but this was later changed to Glen Eira Christian Community Church. We were involved there for several years. John Wall, son of SIM missionaries, was the pastor.

On October 29th Joy went into PANCH hospital in Preston for hand reconstruction surgery. Four plastic joints were put in the knuckles of her left hand and her thumb joint was 'frozen'; pins were inserted to immobilize the thumb until the bones fused.

It was a struggle for the checking team to keep up to schedule, but we thought we could finish work by the end of July 1991. The International Bible Society, who publish the NIV version of the Bible, had agreed to publish two thousand copies for us and pay two thirds of the cost of printing and distribution.

The Boko church continued to grow. Three hundred attended the annual church conference, and the Jesus film was shown in five Boko towns. There were good crowds and many Muslims watched and listened to the simultaneous translation into Boko. Three new churches were built making a total of nineteen.

The boys did well at their exams. Andrew passed his HSC and was granted a place at Monash University to do an Arts course. He wrote the following article at this time:

> While most kids learned to finger paint in kinder, I was herding wild African cattle! Up to the tender age of five I had been brought up in a tiny African village. My parents were missionaries in the sub-Saharan tribe called the Boko, located in the north of Benin.
>
> We came back to Australia when I was five and I started school at Ashburton Primary. In January

1978 I became a Christian. We moved to Sydney in October 1979 where I attended Woolooware Primary. The most vivid memories of my grade prep, one and two are the fact that I was the shortest, and the time I fainted when on detention in grade two!

We returned to Africa in 1980 where I began grade three at Kent Academy boarding school in Nigeria. For seven months of the year my brothers and I were over six-hundred miles from home and Mum and Dad.

These were great years and I learned a tremendous amount about getting on in life and being independent. We returned to Australia in January 1985. This was a new phase of my life. I attended Scotch College in Melbourne and learned to adapt to the Australian system and the all-boy atmosphere. These were perhaps the most formative years of my life, where I learned the facts about not only my school subjects, but also about camping, sports, and my moral development as a gentleman.

I finished my time at Scotch and did well enough to enter arts at Monash University. This year has been a new world all over again.

My experience, as I reminisce, has spanned from the tropics of Africa to the tradition of an old and superb education system at Scotch. Now I find myself competing for marks with many different classes and nationalities. My horizons have been broadened again and will continue to expand as I hope to combine theological studies with my present arts course beginning next year.

I cannot say that studying is a continual thrill, but I know that I am where God wants me, and I can see his plan working through my life. I have many ideas about where my future could lead – perhaps into the ministry, the mission field, the classroom or into the business world. I have confidence however, that God's plan will lead me along the path he wants me to take.

In January 1992 we went on a two-week holiday to Cedar Lake holiday resort in southern Queensland where the boys and I enjoyed activities such as tennis, horse riding, paddle-boating and swimming. I began the year with two jobs. As well as the translation work, I was for the second time SIM Ministry Coordinator in Victoria, working at the SIM office on Monday and Friday mornings. I was also secretary at Caulfield Baptist where attendance had increased to eighty.

Joy was enjoying her new left hand. She had the stainless-steel pins in her thumb for three months. It was operating well, and the four plastic knuckles were excellent. In April the right hand was operated on.

SIL Bible consultant Dr Robert Young had kindly checked the whole Boko Old Testament with me over the last couple of years. He made regular trips from Bendigo and we would meet at Kangaroo Ground. Plans went into turmoil when the missionary who was going to typeset the Bible for us in Benin went home because her mother was dying. Then it was a pleasant surprise for me when I found an SIL man at Kangaroo Ground named Graeme Costin who would do it. I went to Benin in July for the final read-through of the manuscripts. Three men read through their share of the whole Bible, both Old and New Testaments, in seven weeks, and I keyed the corrections into the computer. Another helper checked through the cross references and footnotes. We made many improvements, so much so that the team felt that they should read the manuscript one more time in case they missed something, and because of the probability in making mistakes when I keyed in

corrections. So, the team read it through again during November/
December after I sent them an updated copy. I preached thirty
times in twenty villages while in the Boko area. The Bible School
is bursting at the seams with thirty students and we decided to start
another Bible School at Kalale, forty miles south of Bobena. This
new school would be vital in further opening up the southern half
of the Boko area.

While at Segbana I met Joseph, Igbo by tribe, and converted six
months previously. His faith was a shock to my system. He would
pray nine times a day, fast when he wanted to strengthen his prayers,
and he shared his faith at every opportunity, always prayed for the
sick, and trusted in God for health and protection. When two
Muslim converts were introduced at church, Joseph was so thrilled
he bought each of the Christians who led them to the Lord a crate
of soft drink. When these converts were mentioned at Bible School,
pastors reported ten more Muslim converts. At Saonzi, the Muslim
teacher sold his house and moved out, saying that Christians had
taken over the village.

The Boko translation committee did their final check during
December '91 - February '92, and I typeset the Bible at home
using the Ventura desktop publishing program. Most of the work
involved putting chapter/verse headings at the top of each page and
footnotes at the bottom. Graeme Costin oversaw what I did, and SIL
at Dallas, Texas, did computer tests on the text and then checked
my typesetting. Four Bible maps were prepared and then the laser
printed manuscripts were sent to South Korea for printing. From
there they would be shipped to Benin. The Boko Bible was finally
out of our hands.

Joy continued to have mediocre health, but recommenced her
ministries: two RE classes, Bible class at church, writing for New
Life, leading a SIM prayer meeting, reviewing SIM missionary
candidates and writing letters to supporters. Andrew was accepted
for an Arts/Theology degree, doing Arts at Monash and a Bachelor
of Ministries degree at Ridley. He was helping lead a Bible study
group at Monash and the 7UP youth group at church. Paul was doing

Linguistic Survey
in Nigeria

1992

Fording a swollen stream with motorbike

Work on the Boko Bible was finished and at fifty-two I was in the prime of my professional life; an experienced linguist, Bible translator and lexicographer. For years I had been wondering what I could do next. I loved the challenge of language research. Working out the intricacies of a grammar is like working on a giant jigsaw puzzle or crossword, but many times more complicated. I had taken note of needy language groups in the Pacific because they were closer to home. I also thought about the languages of migrants in Australia whose countries were closed to Christian work, but there was no specific leading from God. On my last trip to Benin, I realized afresh that there were sixty-thousand unreached people just over the border in Nigeria, speakers of Boko and related languages. Although the SIM-related ECWA Church had twenty couples working in the area, they had not affectively reached these people, because they did all their work in the Hausa language. There were no Scriptures available in these Boko-related languages. The Bible Society of Nigeria informed me that no work was being done on these languages and they would welcome a visit from me. An SIL coordinator living in Ilorin one-hundred miles south of the area offered his help.

Having received a green light from the SIM directors concerned, I planned to do a comprehensive survey of the languages later in the year, when I went to Benin for the dedication of the Boko Bible. My vision was to turn these people from darkness to light and from the power of Satan to God by giving them the Scriptures in their own languages. SIL had a program called CADA, Computer Assisted Dialect Adaptation, which enabled one to convert Scriptures from one dialect to another in a fraction of the time it took to translate the original. I could do the initial conversion at home on computer and then go to Nigeria to work through it with mother-tongue speakers. That would not be easy for Joy with her arthritis, but I would ask her to pray about it. SIM Australia were supportive of the new venture, but they told us we would have to get our languishing support level back to one-hundred percent.

Joy found it quite difficult to accept the new project to do yet more translation work. Her health had deteriorated during the past eight years and she wondered whether she could continue to support me in another translation program. My long periods away from home were difficult for her physically. However, she recognized that the boys were growing up and were a wonderful support. She asked the Lord to confirm the new project to her personally, and that he did. I had received a letter from a Nigerian pastor spelling out the specific need of the Bokobaru people for their own Scriptures. He succinctly answered many questions that I had posed. In addition, a message came to Joy from several different sources. The message was: "In acceptance lies peace."

One day while preparing her RE classes, she found a previously unknown song titled: "Let's do it God's way." It went like this:

> Sometimes we don't understand how this could ever
> be his plan,
> but there are reasons that we just can't know.
> I'll remember God can see what's really best for me,
> it's hard times that make us grow.
> I'll do it God's way 'cause his way is the best.
> Yes, and when I start to trust him with the problems
> of each day,
> I'll find out that there's a reason for doing it God's way.

Joy said: "These factors, plus the biblical principle of subjection to the head of the family, made me see clearly that this is right for this time. When I accepted that, a tremendous peace came upon me. Yes, the next few months will still be difficult; for Ross as he goes to Nigeria to do the survey, and for us as we keep the home fires burning. But I have perfect peace in accepting all of this."

Missionary work is a team effort. As well as the necessity of a couple having a united vision, the children have to be considered, and it is impossible for missionaries to do their work without the prayer and financial support of a dedicated team of fellow believers. We were sincerely thankful for sacrificial support by so many for so long.

I was conscious at this time that missionary work is a family effort, especially when Joy and the boys were with me in Benin, but also in those days when I was going to Africa for ten to twelve-week trips. On the one hand there was separation and hardship within the family, on the other hand there were tens of thousands of people living in darkness who needed to hear the gospel. We were thankful for Joy's parents living around the corner. They were always very supportive of the work I was doing, and they helped out in many ways. Who can forget the wonderful roasts and deserts we had every Thursday night when we went to grandma's for dinner? It always smelled so good, and nobody made bread-and-butter pudding, and rice pudding, and flummery, like she did. She used to come around and do all our ironing too.

But I was mostly thankful to Joy for allowing me to take on the projects that I felt God wanted me to do. Without her support the job just wouldn't get done.

I had been filling in part time as SIM Victoria Ministry Coordinator. I was encouraged to take on the role full-time, but I didn't feel gifted for that job, and declined. I was relieved when Phil Short returned from Africa and took over until a permanent person was found.

The dedication of the Boko Bible was delayed until 1993, so I started making preparations to go to Nigeria for the survey during my time there. I knew no one there personally, but I had a copy of a Bokobaru grammar that an SIL missionary had written in the early seventies. In it he mentioned the names of his three language helpers. So, although it was twenty years later, I wrote separate letters to those three people at the only address I could think of, the Kaiama Post Office. I received one reply from Abraham Bata who was a Methodist minister. He told me that one of the three had died in a road accident, and that the other one, Mohammed Haliru, had reverted to Islam, so may not reply. Abraham was very enthusiastic and said that my letter was an answer to his prayers. He had long had the desire to translate the Scriptures into his native tongue and evangelize his own people. I immediately wrote back and asked him to arrange accommodation for me at Kaiama from July 1st.

Doing a linguistic and religious survey of the Borgu area of mid-western Nigeria was quite an adventure. I travelled to Lagos, Nigeria with Balkan Airlines via Zimbabwe, and then took a public taxi to the large city of Ilorin. The taxi was a Peugeot which carried eight passengers. On one trip I sat next to a young man named Dennis. I asked him about his language (Igbo) and his work (he sold medicines), and whether he was a Christian (yes, AOG). Then I said, "How old are you, twenty-three?" "How did you know" he said, "Are you a prophet?" Seizing the opportunity, I said, "I might be, you had better listen to what I'm saying to you." I asked whether he had been baptized ("no"), and what he was doing for Jesus, who had done so much for him ("nothing"). Finally, I asked him whether he had considered going to Bible school to prepare himself for Christian service ("no"). Months later I received a letter from Dennis. He said that when I spoke to him in the taxi, it was if God himself was speaking to him. Imagine my joy when he later came to visit me in New Bussa. He told me he was now baptized and was finishing up with his medicine business. He was on his way home to prepare for Bible school.

At Ilorin I stayed with an SIL administrator named Don Lindholm who was a great help to me over the years. From there I took a taxi to Kaiama where I met Abraham. He was a short sixty-year old man and he had a son named Peter in his early twenties who was very sharp with languages and worked as an electrician. I had arranged for my Boko friends, Levi and Gabriel, to come from Segbana on their motorbikes and meet me at Kaiama from where we would start the survey. I was relieved when they turned up as arranged. Abraham and Peter were keen to help us, and they gave us a lot of information about the churches in the area and the number of Bokobaru villages that surrounded Kaiama. They took us to meet the Emir of Kaiama who was very pleased to meet this white man who had come to promote the language of his people. In a very

143

important voice, he called down all Allah's blessings upon me and my work. It was a white man, colonialist administrator Lord Lugard, who had made his grandfather a first-class Emir. We also greeted the local government officials who welcomed us and said that they were looking to me to produce a Bokobaru script, grammar, dictionary and reading primers for use in their schools.

During the next two weeks Levi and Gabriel, each with a local Bokobaru helper, went to fifteen villages and took down a basic vocabulary list, so that we could ascertain whether they all spoke the same language. We discovered that the Bokobaru spoken in the villages was uniform, but different to the Bokobaru spoken in the main town, Kaiama. Meanwhile Abraham and Peter gave me hundreds of Bokobaru words and helped me work out how Bokobaru grammar differed from Boko grammar. There were nine churches in Kaiama, but their services were held in Hausa and Yoruba languages. They catered for the Christian strangers in town and weren't very interested in reaching the locals, who were Muslim.

After spending two weeks at Kaiama we travelled fifty miles to New Bussa to survey the Bisã speaking people. This was a thriving town of fifteen-thousand inhabitants famous for the fact that it was the headquarters of the Kainji Hydro-electric Scheme which supplies most of Nigeria with its electricity. New Bussa is close to Kainji Dam on the mighty Niger River. Most of the population were strangers and there were twenty-five churches in the town, but not one Bisã adherent. The Bisã section of town surrounded the Emir's palace and no churches were allowed in that area. My friends and I stayed at the White House guest house which was run by a Christian man named Stephen. He was a chef and he prepared nice fish soups which contained the whole fish. My friends ate everything they could pick off the bones and the head. We spent one week taking down wordlists in fifteen Bisã villages which surround New Bussa, including Wawa which had a population of eight-thousand.

On leaving New Bussa we had to travel 125 miles north to the Busa and Kyanga areas. This took us through the area where the

Nigerian Bokos live. In the villages we drove through, we stopped and checked that their language was the same as the Boko in Benin. That was confirmed, except that they have English loanwords, whereas in Benin they have French loanwords. One day we saw a lion on the road about fifty yards ahead, and we stopped abruptly. We waited patiently, and when it disappeared into the bush on the side of the road, we sped past. It was the wet season and there were many streams to cross. In deep streams we had to carry the motorbikes above our heads so that the motors didn't get wet. We had to cross some streams in a canoe. Levi had a relative in one village with whom we stayed overnight.

When we arrived at the Busa town of Illo in the north, we went and greeted the Emir. We explained our mission to him and he allowed us to stay in the Government Guest House which was a rather lavish place, built to accommodate visiting government officials. Levi, Gabriel and I had a king-sized bed to sleep on. We felt we were in the lap of luxury. From there we did language surveys in five Kyanga villages and five Busa villages. In all we collected words on our 227 word-list from forty different villages. We ascertained that Boko, Bokobaru, Bisā and Kyanga were different languages rather than dialects, and each one needed literature and Scriptures in their own tongue. Busa, on the other hand, was close enough to Boko to be regarded as a dialect.

This area of Nigeria is a backwater and one of the least evangelized areas of this large country. We found only seven Bokobaru Christians and two Bisā Christians among eighty-thousand people. The area is Muslim, but the territorial spirits are powerful. Demon possession, witchcraft, spells and moral depravity are rife. The ruling class resisted Islam until the 1920's, when British administration policy encouraged them to embrace it. Although there are numerous churches in Kaiama and New Bussa, they do not reach out to the surrounding indigenous people. There was only one church in the northern area we visited. We had good health, safety on the roads, and were accommodated wherever we went. We thanked God for being with us.

Contact with the Emirs and the local government officials was very positive and encouraging. They were very interested in my proposal to put their languages into writing and prepare booklets for teaching literacy. They offered their full cooperation and said they would teach the children in their primary schools to read and write their own languages.

I employed Abraham and Peter Bata to work with me as from September 1st and I planned to make two six-week trips to Nigeria each year to adapt the Boko Scriptures into their language.

One afternoon Peter and I climbed some towering rocks behind the Emir's palace, so that I could take a photo of Kaiama. Someone had told me that there was a cave somewhere on this rocky outcrop and that a powerful spirit lived there, who had power over the town. Another tor in the Bisã area was called Zenkana after the name of the territorial spirit who lived there. People came from hundreds of miles away to sacrifice to these spirits.

We had been praying for this area and claiming it for Jesus, asking that these evil spirits would be expelled. We remembered the words of Paul: "For our struggle is not against flesh and blood, but against the rulers, against the authorities, against the powers of this dark world and against the spiritual forces of evil in the heavenly realms" (Ephesians 6:12).

On descending the rocks, we had to go past the Emir's palace. He was sitting on the veranda and Peter said: "We had better call in and greet him. He has certainly seen us, and it would be a discourtesy not to greet him." The Emir received us warmly and we soon got chatting about various things. Then I asked him whether he believed that there were powerful spirits living in a cave in the rocks that towered behind his palace. "Oh, yes!" he exclaimed enthusiastically, "They keep a lot of evil away from our town." I was stunned by this response and asked him what the Muslim position was concerning these spirits. He then went on to tell me a story about a beggar who got lost and went into that cave by mistake. He claimed to have seen the spirits praying. "These spirits are Muslims!" the Emir said emphatically. And so, the Muslims continued to sacrifice to them.

Another day I went to greet one of my language helpers, a Muslim school teacher. He told me his sister was very sick in the next room. I went in to see her and prayed for her. My helper said that she was the third wife of her husband, and that the other two had died as a result of witchcraft. This woman was eventually taken to seek help from a witchdoctor, who told them that before they arrived, he knew their problem. "The second-hand mattress you sleep on was stolen, and the true owner put a curse on whoever sleeps on it." They asked him to neutralize the curse so that it would only affect the thief, but before he could do that, she died.

These are the sort of stories you hear in this part of the world and they are firmly believed in by most Christians. How about this one? A Boko man in Benin realized he was one of the poorest in his village, so he went to consult a sorcerer in Nigeria, whom he asked to make him rich. The sorcerer said he must bring him a human head. Back at his village, the man asked his wife to follow him to the river, where, holding a machete, he told her about his trip. The wife quickly took her baby off her back and knelt in the sand and told him not to kill their baby. If he must have a head, he should kill her. She didn't look up until she heard a clanking noise in the sky. There was her husband with arms and legs chained, ascending into the sky. She ran home and told the villagers who came and saw him, now getting smaller and smaller. "Did anyone have a camera", I asked.

Bokobaru and Bisã Translations

1993-2000

Bokobaru and Bisã translation teams

Abraham put in his resignation from the Methodist church, so that he and his son Peter could work on the Bokobaru translation team. He had worked for Wycliffe missionary Klaus Wedekind twenty years previously. After arriving home from Nigeria, I quickly adapted Exodus 1-20, fifty Psalms, Proverbs and Ecclesiastes to Bokobaru, using the vocabulary I had elicited from Abraham and Peter. I posted this material to them and also sent an animal picture booklet, a book of fables and a counting book to the Emirs and some government officials to show them I meant business. Originally, we had thought of producing literature for a combined Bokobaru/Bisã readership, but the government officials in each area preferred literature in their own pure dialect and not a fusion of the two. After some time, we realized that the languages were too far apart, and so I had to adapt the Boko Bible to both Bokobaru and Bisã.

Peter travelled to Ilorin each month to collect their salaries from Don Lindholm and to give a report of the work they had done. They worked up to ten hours a day and started a special prayer meeting for the Bokobaru work.

About this time, I went to the Monash University library, and I was amazed to find how much history was recorded about Borgu, which included the Bokobaru and Bisã areas. As Nigeria was a British colony, there was a lot of information about colonial administration, and memoirs from historiographers. I compiled a forty-page (A4) History of Borgu in English which included charts and maps and pictures, and it proved to be very popular. I later translated it into Bokobaru, Bisã and Boko.

Borgu was an ancient kingdom in mid-western Nigeria, established over one-thousand years ago. It had the reputation that it was never conquered, the Boko/Busa warriors being feared for their horsemanship, their poison arrows and their black magic. A treaty was made with the British colonialists in 1894 and the area became an undeveloped backwater, even by African standards. It measures 60 by 125 miles and had about 200,000 inhabitants of whom 120,000 are Boko/Busa speakers.

The people are basically animist, worshipping territorial spirits. The kingdom of darkness is still very much in evidence with demon possession, black magic used for malevolent purposes, the appeasement of spirits with sacrificial offerings, and many superstitions, charm and taboos. After resisting Islam for centuries, the local kings became Muslim around 1930, and they were soon followed by the influential people in the area, and eventually by most of the village people.

At the end of 1992 Andrew averaged credits for his Arts and Theology subjects and Paul passed his VCE and applied for a music degree course. Matthew and Peter moved up to years eleven and nine respectively. Joy's health was of continuing concern. The cartilage in her right knee collapsed and hampered her walking. She didn't like going out unless really necessary. Getting in and out of the car was a hassle as was getting up from a chair. Her surgeon, Mr. John Harris, suggested a knee replacement.

Andrew saved up for his ticket and went with me to Nigeria in February. He was born in Nigeria and wanted to see his old school there, which he did while I worked at Kaiama. He travelled to Jos with my Bokobaru helper, Peter, and stayed a few days at Kent Academy. He met many SIM missionaries and talked about work opportunities.

I presented my suggested script for writing Bokobaru and Bisā to the literacy committees and looked for a Bisā worker, finally deciding on a thirty-year old budding politician named Mohammed Gimba. Then I spent a week with Abraham and Peter going through the gospel of Mark in Bokobaru. That exercise gave them a better appreciation of translation methods, and it gave me a better understanding of Bokobaru. I bought Peter a second-hand motorbike for visiting the villages and helped Abraham find a new home, as he had to move from the Methodist manse.

Andrew and I arrived in Segbana in time for the Boko Church Conference, including the dedication of the Boko Bible. There were four-hundred Boko there, and fifteen SIM missionaries came for the dedication, together with Benin church representatives and local officials. After all the talking 250 Bibles were sold and everyone went home rejoicing in their new possession. In the capital Cotonou, I was interviewed in French on national television, because the Boko Bible was the first Bible to be completed in Benin. My Nigerian project was accepted as a SIMaid project because of the emphasis on literacy. Tax-deductible projects have to be humanitarian in nature, not religious. It had an annual budget of $20,000.

After our return to Australia Joy had her knee operation which was a great success. She said that joint was now the best one in her body. Someone gave me a Macintosh PowerBook and I busied myself transferring all my files to it. For the Scripture adaptation I used an SIL program called Interlinear Text (IT). I was now adapting the Boko gospels of Matthew and Luke to Bokobaru and Bisã. I prepared phonologies, which described the sound systems of those languages, and also translated the reading primers and commenced work on dictionaries.

Apart from the translation work, our aim for the Bokobaru area was twofold. In the area of evangelism, Abraham and Peter would plant a church at Sirigberia, a Bokobaru village where there was a potential following of seventy. I would encourage the Boko church in Benin to release some men to come and work in the Kaiama area. As for literacy, the local government said we had their full co-operation for a literacy program. Abraham would form a Bokobaru Literacy committee which would include the Emir, Mohammed Haliru, and representatives from the Emirate Council, the local government, the education department, adult education department, and the primary schools. They love committees, but unfortunately, the members are chosen because of prestige and not their ability to get the job done.

In 1994, while I was chatting with the Emir of Kaiama, Alhaji Mohammed Tukur Omar, he told his umbrella steward to bring out the royal umbrella. It had been given to his grandfather in 1898 by Lord Lugard, a colonial administrator, who is called the father of modern Nigeria. Despite its age, it was still being used on official occasions. It was red and domed with gold tassels all around. It measured eight feet across and stood eight feet high. The Emir asked me if it would be possible for me to procure him a similar umbrella, as this one was getting a bit shabby.

I thought this would be a wonderful PR opportunity, so I decided to buy one for him as a gift and made enquiries in Australia. There were many cheap market umbrellas from Asia, but the only one suitable for a king was one made in Seaford, Victoria. At $600 the bright red acrylic umbrella had a good chance of lasting as long as its predecessor.

The pole didn't fold, so the next problem was how to carry this forty-pound, eight-foot box ten-thousand miles around the world to Kaiama in Nigeria. The first 9,600 miles was easy. I checked it in at Melbourne airport and then picked it up at the Lagos airport. My problems began with an electrical storm in London. The plane had taken off two hours late and arrived in Lagos late.

The Bible Society guest house man who came to meet me at the airport gave up after a time, but he left some Nigerian staff to look for me. It was a bit hard to sneak through customs with an eight-foot package, so I was soon shunted off to a corner of the airport to deal with customs officials. They sent me off to an office quite a distance away, where they worked out the duty I would have to pay. It took two hours of filling in forms and running backwards and forwards between customs officials before I was able to pay the forty percent duty. It was then that the guest house staff found me and phoned their boss. I was startled by his response: "Tell him I will pick him up at six a.m.!" It was approaching midnight and the streets of Lagos were too dangerous to travel at that hour. I lay down on a seat in the luggage collection area and was thankful for the lights, air conditioning, lack of mosquitoes, and the security man at the door.

Usually when travelling the two-hundred miles from Lagos to Ilorin I paid $4 and squeezed into a Peugeot 504 with seven or eight other passengers, but with my big parcel I lashed out and hired the taxi for $40. The driver took me to where I was staying in Ilorin. At Ilorin I had additional luggage: four big typewriters I had imported for the literacy programs and three bicycles I had bought for evangelists. A fellow worker in the Lord's service was going my way and we packed it all together with the umbrella into his pick-up. Thankfully the soldiers and customs officials along the road didn't ask us to unpack.

My host in Kaiama organized a date for me and my fellow workers to present the umbrella to the Emir. After waiting outside the palace for ten minutes, we were asked to come in. Imagine my surprise when I found one hundred officials gathered to witness the presentation. In was the Gaani festival and any Bokobaru man of importance was back in town to celebrate it. Most of the people there were Alhajis, people who had made the pilgrimage to Mecca. After everyone was introduced, the Imam was asked to open in prayer, and then I was introduced and asked to speak.

I greeted them in their language to break down barriers caused by their having a Christian missionary in their midst, and then I thanked the Emir for his welcome and friendliness over the past three years. I related the Emir's conversation to me about the umbrella and said that as the first umbrella had been given by a white man nearly one-hundred years ago, it was appropriate that another white man should replace it.

We went out into the courtyard where we erected the new umbrella, and I presented it to the Emir. The Emir responded with a gracious speech in which he praised the white man, who unlike the first one, had brought a gift with "no strings attached." He stressed the fact that this missionary had shown them he was serious about helping them.

Many speeches followed in which people praised me for putting their language into writing, enabling their people to become literate in their own language. An immigration official from Lagos stood up and said: "I want Mr. Jones to know that whenever he is passing through Lagos, he will never have any problems with immigration." Then a customs official stood and made the same declaration.

We went back inside the palace where food and drinks were served to all the guests. After a Christian guest was asked to close in prayer, the federal assistant police inspector said with a smile, "You can see that we have religious tolerance here. You can now feel free to convert the convertible!"

In 1994 I came into contact with European Economic Community (EEC) personnel who ran an adult education program in the middle belt of Nigeria. I was invited to go to Ilorin to see Professor Oyedeji who headed up this Middle Belt program. As a result of that interview, the EEC said they would now teach adults in the Kaiama and Borgu Local Government Areas to read and write in their own languages: Boko, Bokobaru and Bisã, rather than in English and Hausa. I was appointed the official writer for the EEC in these languages, which meant I would oversee all literature being produced in these languages. There was the potential for thousands of people learning to read and write these languages and being exposed to the Scriptures I was translating. That was exciting. Contracts were finalized in the three languages and the EEC printed ten-thousand booklets in each language for the literacy programs. I arranged with the Emirs to have the official launchings of the literacy programs on my next trip in August.

The Bokobaru literacy launching took place at the council chambers of the Kaiama Local Government Secretariat. About two-hundred people were present, mainly officials and dignitaries who had been invited, including about twenty EEC officials from Ilorin. After many speeches, including one from myself, two Bokobaru stood up and read stories from the reading primers and then wrote some words on the blackboard to illustrate how the language was written. A praise singer with calabash accompaniment spent fifteen minutes praising everyone involved and in the traditional way many people pressed hundreds of naira, the Nigerian currency, onto his sweating forehead.

At New Bussa several hundred people gathered by the Emir's palace for a similar program. The Emir of Borgu, the chairman and secretary of the Borgu Local Government, village and district heads, traditional rulers, state and local education officials were all present. I presented typewriters to the chairman of the local government, to be used for Bisã and Boko literacy. Both occasions were looked upon as historic, an opportunity to banish illiteracy and improve the quality of people's lives. Our work was appreciated, as expressed in a keynote address which went something like this: Once more to Mr Jones and his able teammates who are God sent, words cannot adequately express our delight and appreciation, for they simply brought light. May God bless them and reward them abundantly here and beyond. His teammates have done their kiths and kins proud. May God bless them and reward them all abundantly, here and beyond.

The following year we trained some instructors at literacy workshops, but then, suddenly, disappointment! The EEC program closed down in protest against alleged human rights violations in Nigeria. No more booklets would be printed, and the instructors wouldn't teach without being paid, so the literacy program lost its momentum. There were many promises by local officials, but if there was no financial incentive, they were not really interested, especially a program run by Christians.

In January 1996, I flew to Nigeria and started working formally with the Bokobaru and Bisā translation teams. Working eight to nine hours a day, six days a week, we were able to check the twelve books we had prepared. We first corrected the adaptation of Bokobaru and then worked on Bisā. The Bisā workers were guided by the comments of the Bokobaru workers and vice versa. On Sunday, I participated in evangelization in the villages with some of my workers.

At New Bussa I helped Mohammed Tanko to build a simple office in his compound which was basically a cement floor and a corrugated iron roof with low mud walls. His Muslim brothers complained to the Emir that we had built a church in their family compound, and the Emir ordered it to be dismantled. I wanted to confront the Emir over the matter but was advised not to. The Emirs always appeared to be cooperative, but there was no freedom of religion. They would do their best to hinder the spread of the gospel, and they openly threatened any of their own subjects who showed interest in becoming Christians.

We prepared nine booklets in each of the three languages and printed two-hundred copies of each, 5,400 in all. This was the first time Scripture was printed in Bokobaru and Bisā. We divided Genesis up into six booklets entitled: Adam, Noah, Abraham, Isaac, Jacob and Joseph, and also printed Ecclesiastes, an animal fable book and a counting book. They all sold for the subsidized price of fifteen to thirty cents each. We worked on the three dictionaries paying special attention to the tones and checked five-thousand words in each, up to 'y'; we couldn't quite finish before I left.

On arriving home, I wrote a paper called: "Logophoricity Redefined – the case of Boko" which was published in the Monash University Linguistic Papers. In November I attended a conference for Bible translators at the SIM headquarters in Charlotte, North Carolina, USA. SIM translators were working on over twenty languages in eight countries We learnt about the latest computer technology produced by SIL. I had thoughts of becoming a translation consultant. All I needed to qualify was a time of apprenticeship – but it never eventuated.

Back among the Bokobaru, Peter and Isaac were having success in their evangelistic activities. One church had been established at Sirigberia, and now people were responding at Kugizi. The chief of Kugizi was a very gracious man, over eighty years old. He still worked on his farm and was pleased with a pair of glasses I gave him. I gave away forty pairs of glasses to older people who couldn't read without them.

When visiting the Emir of Kaiama, I asked if I could come back the following week and preach to him and his executive council. He agreed and the following week I arrived and announced that I was going to open their eyes. After fitting everyone with a pair of standard reading spectacles I spoke to them about the Kingdom of God. I gave them all a copy of the message and to the Emir I gave copies of twenty tracts I had prepared about Jesus with the Muslim world view in mind.

Joy had a troublesome shoulder and when the surgeon looked at the X-rays, he doubted that he could do anything to help, it was one of the worst shoulders he had seen. After a trip to USA he said there was a titanium prosthesis he could put in, but the new joint proved to be only a partial success. Blood tests showed that Joy had an over active thyroid and she was given a precise dose of radioactive iodine to destroy much of her thyroid gland. Unfortunately, it destroyed it completely and she had to add thyroid tablets to the large number of medications she was taking. She also had to have nine teeth extracted – no end to her medical problems!

A Nigerian prophet called Martin Luther came to Kaiama, and despite the fact that there were ten churches in town, he declared that Kaiama was still chained, the pastors had climbed in under the chain, they had not broken it. When he came to the roundabout, he looked at it and declared it to be evil. He didn't know, but ten years beforehand a live cow was buried under the roundabout, a sacrifice to the local spiritual powers. Kaiama is named after a territorial spirit, called Kaama in Bokobaru, who lives in a small hut in the bush. The prophet prayed for Peter's mother and broke the demonic oppression that had been bothering her. The transformation in the life of his mother convinced me that he was genuine.

When in Nigeria the translation teams would spend half the time at Kaiama and half at New Bussa. I wanted to have contact with the local Bokobaru and Bisã peoples, because my vision was not only to give them the Scriptures and teach them literacy so that they could read it, but also to start churches in these two language groups. Because of Muslim persecution, it was extremely difficult for people to make a decision to follow Jesus and then persevere. One day, G. came to visit me at New Bussa. He had been baptized six years before, but had been up and down since then, mainly down, because of persecution. He had his certificates and belongings confiscated by his family and he was finally driven out of his uncle's home. His wife was taken from him by her Muslim family. He had been going to church on and off and had no money and few friends. I took him to two churches on Sunday and at each church someone came up and offered to help him.

Sabo was in a similar position and was too afraid to make a clear stand for the Lord. He was not married and worked as a security officer. He was also a boy-scout leader. I took him on as a worker to encourage him, but it didn't last.

B. came to visit me at the White House guest inn one day. My worker Mohammed Tanko had lent him a Bible and had had some discussions with him. He had first heard about Jesus through Bible Knowledge classes at secondary school. "Is it true that Jesus died for the sins of the whole world?" he asked excitedly. I directed him to John 1:29 where John the Baptist on seeing Jesus, said to his disciples: "Look, the Lamb of God, who takes away the sin of the world!" We had a good discussion. Then he took me to his household which was quite close to the Emir's palace and showed me a certain building. "This is our guesthouse," he said. "Whenever you come in future, you won't stay at the White House, you'll stay with me." I thought that it would be nice to have a Bisã person as my host, rather than staying at a commercial place. However, I didn't see B. again. When I enquired about him, I was told that he had gone to buy fish on the other side of the country. Eventually I heard that his family had forbidden him to see me again and he had bowed to their wishes.

Another disappointment I had on that trip was a robbery; I lost $830. The money was in my bag when I arrived in New Bussa and stayed at the White House for two nights. I didn't check it and the next day we went down to Kaiama where I was going to put the money in the bank. I was staying in a room with Samuel, one of my workers. When I looked to check my money, I discovered it was gone. I alerted Samuel and other co-workers and they eventually discovered that the thief had opened a side pocket of my bag and cut through into the locked main part of the bag with a knife. We didn't know whether the money had been stolen in Kaiama or back in New Bussa. As only my workers had been in the room in Kaiama, suspicion fell on the manager (not the owner) of the White House, who had a record with the police for stealing. I heard that the police gave him their treatment. They hung him from a rafter by his legs and beat his bare backside, telling him to confess, which he didn't do. Another time that I lost money was when the bank in Kaiama went broke. It was just before I was about to leave, and I went to the bank to draw wages for my workers. The door was locked and never opened again. That time I lost $1500 and my workers were not happy.

One day while staying at the White House, I met Mohamed, the younger brother of the proprietor. I talked to him about Jesus and later his brother said, "If you invite Mohamed to go to church tomorrow, I think he will go with you." He did, and when we arrived back home, he asked me how he could become a Christian. We have been good friends ever since.

I heard about the possibility of dubbing the Jesus film or the whole of Luke's gospel onto video and thought it was a great idea. I never wanted to pass up opportunities like that. The translation team thought a narrator approach would be better than multiple voices and we chose one speaker for each of the three languages and gave them the scripts so that they could practice fitting the dialogue into the correct timing of each scene. Levi came from Benin and five us went to Jos for a month to dub the four-hour twenty-minute video in each language. A Wycliffe couple did the technical work. The cost of recording them and for three projectors I bought was $10,000. The projectors which worked off car batteries didn't last long, but we did sell videos to the wealthier people who had video players. Twenty years later the videos were converted to a better format with improved color and sound and are still being used.

In 1998 the adaptation of the New Testament into Bokobaru and Bisã was completed, but another twelve months was needed to check through the twenty-seven books. PhD research had uncovered many hidden secrets in the grammar and tonology of the languages leading to greater accuracy. In 1998 I got my first email address and marveled at how easy and cheap it was to communicate with people by email all over the world.

I was given a new job within SIM, to be the International Translation Coordinator. That meant attending international translation seminars each year. I had oversight of the twenty-five translation projects SIM missionaries were doing around the world and my job was to give them technical support. I began a newsletter for them called SIMphonics. In 1999 I attended the Bible Forum at Fort Lauderdale in Florida. This was a fellowship of seventeen agencies involved in Bible translation and distribution. Most of the delegates were leaders of their organizations and I felt like a fish out of water. I was a grassroots worker, not an administrator. Nevertheless, I maintained this role for several years.

PhD Studies

---◆---

1995-1997

Ross and Andrew
PhD in Linguistics and BA in Arts
Monash University 2nd December 1998

Fearing that my research on the Boko, Bokobaru and Busa languages would only be of profit to termites, mice and cockroaches, I went to Monash University in Clayton to see if it would be possible for me to do a Masters in Linguistics so that my thesis on Boko grammar would be available to someone, somewhere. Pharmacy was my main academic qualification and in 1963, that was only a diploma. The heads of the linguistics department asked to see some of my linguistic work. After examining it, they said if I could produce work like that, they would accept me as a PhD candidate, not on the basis of my qualifications, but for the extensive research experience I had had in Africa.

I really enjoyed doing my PhD. There is a need in comparative linguistics to have comprehensive descriptions of new languages, so I was encouraged to give a full overview of the phonemics and grammar of the Boko/Busa language cluster with special attention given to interesting areas of the languages. During the first year I worked over the Boko material I had gathered during the past twenty-five years in Benin Republic. Not having a primary degree in linguistics, I had to do a lot of reading to get a better grasp of linguistic terminology and issues. The previous linguistic education I had had to this point were the two SIL courses I had done in Brisbane and in UK.

Most PhD students struggle to get their thesis written in three years, but I had no trouble. Right from the beginning I knew what I wanted to do, and I was highly motivated to do a good job of it. Secondly, this kind of research is right up my alley. It is what I was born for! The university was only five miles from my home and I only had to go there two days a week. I was spending half of my time on the Bokobaru and Bisā translation adaptations. And then I had a very good supervisor, which is a very important factor when doing a PhD. Dr Heather Bowe gave me at least one hour of her time every Friday afternoon. She read through everything I wrote and told me what I needed to redo. I used a computerized language description questionnaire as the basic structure for my work. This ensured that it was comprehensive. During the first year I rewrote all the data I had on Boko, refining the linguistic terminology and highlighting the characteristic features of Boko. I explained differences the Bokobaru and Bisã grammars had with the Boko grammar.

In the second year I went through the whole thing again, filling in the gaps and enlarging on interesting areas. Similarly, in the third year, I went through the whole thesis again fine-tuning it. The final product was 510 pages.

I didn't have to pay any fees at Monash except for the student fees of $170 a year. Monash, on the other hand gave me a conference travel fund grant which enabled me to attend a conference in Germany where I presented a paper on "The Ethnic Groups of Present Day Borgu". This was knowledge I had gained on the language survey trip. I also received two overseas study grants during my candidature and made two trips to Nigeria to complete my research.

Without bothering you with the many pages of typos and minor errors that my examiners found in my thesis I will quote from the glowing reports they made. First, the report from Dr P Peterson, University of Newcastle, NSW.

> The stated aim of the author is to present a detailed and comprehensive description of the languages of the Boko/Busa language cluster in a form that is maximally accessible to other linguists. In this he has succeeded admirably. The thesis contains a wealth of material at all levels of linguistic analysis. Sometimes there is a danger that the reader will be overwhelmed by the mass of detail provided; however, in general the author has managed to present his material sufficiently clearly.

> I was particularly impressed with the author's ability to present an orderly account of the extremely complex and pervasive tonological system which is a feature of the language cluster. Indeed, there is sufficient

material in this area alone to serve as a thesis topic in its own right.

There is no doubt that this thesis makes a significant contribution to knowledge of the languages of this area and will increase our understanding of such phenomena as logophoricity. I have no hesitation in recommending the acceptance of this thesis for the degree of Doctor of Philosophy.

The second examiner was well known linguist Professor Bernard Comrie from the University of Southern California, USA. He wrote:

The thesis in question is a significant contribution to knowledge because of the detail and analytical skill with which the description of Boko/Busa grammar is carried out. It is comprehensive, covering phonology, morphology and all the major syntactic constructions of the language. For what is in effect the first grammar of a little studied language it is astonishingly detailed, indeed the fine level of many of the observations is of the kind normally associated with grammars of languages that have been studied by a succession of linguists. The author has also succeeded in drawing out those aspects of the grammar of Boko/Busa that are particularly relevant for current issues in linguistic theory, which makes the thesis a significant contribution to the understanding of the subject with which it deals.

I will cite just one example to show the ways in which the thesis satisfies the twin criteria of descriptive adequacy and theoretical insight. Chapter eight on Logophoricity on its own would satisfy the criterion of demonstrating the candidate's capacity to carry

out independent research, and the criterion of
presenting material worthy of publication. Indeed, I
hope the author would consider both publishing the
thesis as a whole, taking into account any suggested
improvements by readers, and taking some of the
theoretically most interesting parts, such as the
discussion on logophoricity, and developing them
further as separate journal articles.

I did take his advice and my thesis was published by Lincom
Europa in Germany as part of their series: Lincom Studies in African
Linguistics. Through their distribution center my thesis is now found
in the hands of many linguists and in university libraries all over
the world, which was my original desire. An extra bonus to writing
this thesis was that the educated Boko people, and especially those
interested in their language, were impressed by the fact that their
tribe and language were now on the world map, spoken about and
studied in the world's universities. They never cease to thank me for
that.

Launching Bokobaru and Bisã Scriptures

2001-2004

**My speech at the launching of the Bokobaru
Bible outside the Emir's palace**

A Boko pastor named Philip came from Benin with his wife and child to begin ministry in the Bokobaru village of Kanikoko. I had spent time with the old chief over a few years and he was impressed by Christian teaching. When a meningitis epidemic killed twenty-five people in his village, another Christian group came and prayed specifically for the epidemic to stop. After their prayer, there were no more deaths, so this strengthened his positive view of Christianity. When we wanted to build a church, he gave us land and a church was built, but when the Emir heard about it, he sent people to pull off the doors and windows, and he demoted the chief. State security officers were informed and called in to look at the situation. They warned the Emir not to harass the Christians, but the Emir had a tight hold on his people.

Philip moved to another village called Kugizi, and three Evangelical Missionary Society (EMS) missionaries arrived and settled with their families in other Bokobaru villages. They were all planting churches, so there was a total of eight churches started in the last few years.

Philip's life illustrates how Christianity spreads in Africa, and how God calls people into Christian service. When he was seventeen, he was a Muslim and he had a friend who was a Quranic teacher. He used to teach him to read the Quran, and one day he told him there was another way, and the people that take that way are sure to find paradise, but they can only marry one wife. Philip asked him how he could know more about that way, and the teacher told him that his friend Jeremy was in it. Philip felt very happy about that, so that night, he waited for Jeremy by the village well. When he saw him, he started an argument with him and said: "How come you found a good way and you didn't tell me about it." Jeremy responded: "What are you talking about?" Philip said: "The Jesus way." Jeremy told him to forgive him, then we went into his house and brought out a little booklet and read it to Philip. It said that Jesus was the way to heaven. Philip was extremely happy about what he heard. Jeremy told him to pray to God and Philip told him he didn't know how to pray, so Jeremy prayed for him.

At that time Jeremy was attending high school at Kalale. Whenever he returned home on Saturday, he and Philip would climb up a big rock and pray, and Philip would learn how to read Boko and then they would pray for people, that they might trust in Jesus. Philip had a good friend named Alhaji Zwanaobe. When he talked to him about Jesus, he repented.

Philip had a fiancée who was ready to marry, but his in-laws said that if he didn't give up Christianity, they would not allow her to marry him. This caused a lot of difficulties, and the village people rose up against the Christians who had become quite numerous. Philip left there and went to work in Nigeria for six years. His fiancée waited for him for a while and then married someone else. While in Nigeria he attended a short-term Bible School.

This is how Jesus called him into service. In a dream he saw that he had gone to work at the farm, and on returning he saw that he was very dirty. Then he saw an expanse of water spread out in front of him. He thought: "I'll go immediately and wash myself in that water." When he entered the water, it came up to his knees, then he thought: "I'll go in further." Then the water came up to his waist. Then he went in further. Just then he slipped on the mud and the water swallowed him up, he couldn't stand. He rose to the surface and sank again. The third time he came up, he opened his mouth and called out to Jesus to save him. Then he saw someone come from heaven dressed in white. He took him by his hand and lifted him up out of the water. When his foot left the water, he woke up.

He had a second dream while in Nigeria. A pastor had called him to come to his village to help him make some cement blocks. One night while there, he dreamt he was in an arid land, then he saw something like a well. He was going to look at it, and he could hear people crying out in that pit. He could see fire and smoke, and then he saw the arms and legs of people sticking up like those of dead animals. When he saw this, he was really frightened. As he stood there watching, he heard a voice saying: "What do you see there?" He said he didn't know what it was. Then the voice said to him: "These people that you see are people who haven't believed

171

in Jesus." He tried to turn his head to see who was talking to him, but his head refused to turn. Then he disappeared. It was during the cold season, but when he woke up, he was perspiring and very frightened. During the early morning prayer meeting, he related his dream to the pastor, and he told him that God was calling him into his service.

When he departed to his home town, the Christians told him to enter Bible School at Kalale. He got married in 1995 and in 1998 he went to Kugizi in Nigeria as a missionary. The things that he saw gave him great strength.

In January '99 five church leaders came from Jos to survey the Boko/Bokobaru/Bisã area. They promised to send eight new EMS missionaries. When they showed the Jesus film in Hausa in the Boko area, one hundred people responded. When I asked one young man whether he was going to follow Jesus, he said: "Would my father allow it?" (In other words, "No!")

Five new missionaries arrived in the Bokobaru area in May making a total of eleven. Seven of them had churches to pastor, the other four planned to build churches in their villages in the dry season. Christians in those villages numbered five-hundred including sixty Bokobaru. I had to help these missionaries out financially, because often their wages ($30 month) came from HQ late, and sometimes the wages were six months in arrears. I also financed Mohammed Shero and EMS missionary Isaac to do theology certificates at Igbaja theological seminary and another two Bokobaru youth to attend Hausa Bible School. There was so much poverty that I didn't know where to start, but when I saw someone wanting to make progress spiritually, I was always ready to help him.

The translation teams finished the Bokobaru and Bisã New Testaments and we contacted the Bible Society of Nigeria, who said they would be happy to publish our work subject to checking by their translation consultant. We also completed all 150 Psalms and worked on the History of Borgu booklet. We moved our base from Mohammed Haliru's house to an air-conditioned guest inn at $8 a day. I finally decided to add fifty percent of the Old Testament to the

New Testaments in Bokobaru and Bisã to give us sixty-two percent of the Bible.

My workers were not always reliable. One year when I arrived in New Bussa, my main Bisã worker Issa was sick with malaria, my second worker had been arrested for possession of Indian hemp and was in prison, and my third worker Usman had decided to take off and further his studies. The Bokobaru team of four was strong, but Abraham had recurring blood pressure problems, and was not able to contribute much after the first week. Haliru was thrown off a motorbike taxi, when the driver failed to miss a large hole, and he had a day off to recover from abrasions and bruising. On another occasion two workers were sick with typhoid.

We finished translating fifty percent of the Old Testament in 2001. There was still final checking to do, computer tests, consultant checking and then the typesetting. After disappointing us twice, a representative from the Bible Society of Nigeria came and asked many questions about the languages and translation teams. I met the General Secretary in Lagos on my way home. He said they were happy to publish our Scriptures, but I would have to finance the project. Small languages in a Muslim area with newly developed churches weren't going to be financially viable. So, I worked out a budget and wrote up a SIM project. We decided on printing one-thousand copies in each language for $7 each. They would be printed in Nigeria at a printer who had done satisfactory work for the Bible Society. The consultant only did a few week's work with us before giving his approval. There were also the three dictionaries to prepare for publication. They were to be published by Lincom Europa at no cost to us. The manuscript files were sent to Germany in August 2004. The dictionaries were approximately three-hundred pages each and defined about seven-thousand words each.

We planned to have two launching ceremonies at New Bussa and Kaiama in October '04. We could have had dedication ceremonies and invited all the churches to come, but most of the Christians in these towns come from other parts of Nigeria and speak different languages. It wasn't those people that we wanted to impact. These

Scriptures were for the Bisã and Bokobaru people and we wanted them to be involved and to know that this literature was now available in their languages. So, I visited the Emir of Kaiama and he agreed for us to launch the literature at the entrance to his palace. That would give it prestige and attract the leaders of Bokobaru society. We organized it so that that the SIM Borgu Language Project and the local government's Department of Adult Education would be the joint sponsors. Invitations were sent out to all the leading government officials, village chiefs, pastors and school principals.

I had read Rick Warren's book, 'The Purpose Driven Life', and had heard about his famous Saddleback Church in California, so I was excited when I received an email from a leader of their mission team. They had visited New Bussa and wanted to adopt it as a town that they could give financial and spiritual support to. He said he sensed that the Lord was about to do something special in New Bussa after the launching and they wanted to be part of it. The SIM Nigeria director also planned to attend, and also my son Matthew.

Jenni Beadle of SIL helped me typeset the Scriptures using PageMaker, but we still hadn't heard from the United Bible Societies in Nairobi who were to give their approval to proceed with the printing. Five months were lost because the Nigerian consultant didn't send the manuscripts to Nairobi. He hadn't been given a copy of the memorandum of understanding that we had so carefully nutted out! The launchings were postponed to January 2005 and later rescheduled for March.

How can I describe the month of March in Nigeria? I found it a very difficult time, but it was good to have Matthew with me. He is used to backpacking and never complained about the conditions and was a great help. The difficulties experienced included travelling two-thousand miles over dusty roads in crowded taxis in extreme heat. I got dehydrated at one stage, I had a short bout of dysentery, and I went home with a sinus infection. Then there were the meetings with the local government officials, being sent from one office to the next with the suspicion that nobody knew what was going on, and the apprehension of not knowing whether the literature launchings would be properly supported and organized. Both in New Bussa and Kaiama the officials changed the dates I had originally suggested, so that we ended up having the launchings on Good Friday and Easter Sunday mornings.

Five hundred invitations had been printed for each launching and delivered personally by Christian helpers. In New Bussa the new Emir was impressed with the efforts made to promote the Bisã language and he was amazed that I had spent thirty-six years working in Borgu. He threw his support behind the launching, but it was communicated to me that he wouldn't be able to launch the Bible with the other literature, as the Emir had enemies looking for something to accuse him of – like promoting the Bible in a state where Sharia law was in force.

When I first instigated these launchings, I didn't realize that it was a Nigerian custom for the launchers to buy copies of the literature at high prices as a reward for the author. The chief launcher at New Bussa was the speaker of the House of Representatives from the State capital of Mina. After his speech, he launched the literature with the sum of ten-thousand naira, in those days equivalent to US$100. The Emirate Council also pledged $100 while three local governments in the area pledged $50 each. In all thirty-five people came to the microphone and pledged over $500. This was an unexpected bonus, but not much was given in cash, and when I appointed an agent to collect the pledges, the small amount collected was kept by him for his expenses!

In Kaiama we were thrilled to hear that all the Bokobaru elite were back in town for the Easter break and would attend the launching. On Easter morning my workers, friends and guests waited to be called to the palace, but didn't get called until 2 p.m. A couple of SIM missionaries from Jos and a representative of the Bible Society of Nigeria were in attendance, as well as our friends from the Saddleback Church in California, but in the end the crowd at Kaiama was disappointing. Many of the elite were too busy with discussions and didn't attend. The Emir was not well and stayed indoors. Eleven people made pledges to a total of $400.

But the encouraging thing was that I could talk about the Bible. In my speech I mentioned that the Bible consists of Ataura, Zabur and Injil, names used by Muslims for books sent down by God – the Law, the Psalms and the Gospel. I reminded them that the Quran said that Muslims must believe in all the books sent down by God, so this Bible was not just for Christians, but for everyone. The MC of the occasion held a Bokobaru Bible up in his hand and repeated much of what I had said. Then one wag in the audience cried out: "Maybe he can translate the Quran for us!"

One hundred gift packs of literature including the Bible were given to the people making pledges and the other dignitaries. Education officials in both New Bussa and Kaiama said they would make sure that the literacy materials were used in all local primary schools. I didn't hear confirmation of this until 2011 when an official phoned me to say that they had finally decided to implement that promise.

The Bisã Bibles had a Christian dedication in an evening service at the ECWA church in New Bussa, while the Bokobaru Bibles were dedicated at a Christian celebration in a Bokobaru village. 17,500 pieces of literature had been printed, the fruit of twelve years of work: Bibles, dictionaries, histories and literacy materials. We were pleased with the quality of the printing of all these booklets except the Bibles. We had to go through all two thousands of them and we rejected one hundred copies that had damaged text, blank pages or upside-down covers.

Following is an article that Joy wrote for New Life Christian Newspaper at this time, 19th October 1995, called, "A different life".

> As the wife of an ever-busy Bible translator who commutes to Nigeria twice a year, I would like to comment on a lifestyle with a difference – mine! In January 1985 our whole family returned from Benin, West Africa, for the high school education of our four sons. The Boko people of Benin had their New Testament, but my husband, Ross, wanted them to

experience a whole Bible. He decided to continue translation at home and travel to Benin for ten to twelve weeks each year to work with his translation team. For six years he did this, and the Bible was completed. Now the Boko people are enjoying their Bible.

After the Boko Bible was complete, Ross wondered what to do next. He took a trip to Nigeria to research the language groups and people across the border from where we had worked in Benin. That was an amazing time, and we saw God's hand at work as people co-operated with him wherever he went in this strongly Muslim area. They welcomed him and his proposed translations into their languages. Since then things have moved on well. Now he goes twice a year for six or seven weeks and is doing a literacy program together with a European Economic Community aid project. Two Bibles in the related Bisã and Bokobaru languages are more than a quarter done. Ross uses an excellent computer program for the adaptation.

In July when Ross left for seven weeks, a physiotherapist at my hydrotherapy class said: "I'd be dark on my husband if he went away for seven weeks." I responded that I believe in what he's doing, so it's OK. No, non-Christian people don't understand our lifestyle, and our commitment to get two more Bibles translated.

Our minister asked Ross to send a fax when in Nigeria, but Ross' reply was: "Even my wife doesn't hear from me for weeks when I go to Nigeria." That's how it is. Faxes don't work, and mail doesn't come. On August 2nd Ross posted us a card. He arrived home on September 13ᵗʰ, and the card came on the 29ᵗʰ! Phones are unavailable in the bush area where he does his work. If he comes out to a city and the phones are working, he rings. Last trip I didn't hear for five weeks. So, what do I do? Daily I pray for his health, safety and protection, and then I purposefully refuse to worry as that accomplishes nothing. I then get on with my life, worry free.

While Ross is away, our four sons are supportive and help me tremendously. Because they all love the Lord and are supportive of his ministry, they do their practical bit. So, it's a family thing and we all thank God for what he is doing in Nigeria. To know God's will and to do it is all that really matters. Even though our life has many comings and goings, a deep peace and joy about it all makes it worthwhile.

The following report was written by Bill Foute, Director of SIM Nigeria, in Intercom, issue 177, November-December 2005, and entitled: "Now I know God speaks our language."

Three languages – Boko, Bisã, and Bokobaru – are not tongue twisters, but God's marvelous work. God has used Dr Ross Jones to help three related language groups say for the first time: "I never knew God spoke our language." Way over along the western border of Nigeria reside the Bokobaru and Bisã people. They are related to the Boko people of Benin Republic. Ross, an Australian SIMer, worked for twenty-five years to bring God's Word to the Boko people along with the good news that God loves them and has provided a way for them to be forgiven. After completing the Bible for the Boko people, Ross began making trips from Australia to Nigeria to bring God's Word to their relatives on the Nigerian side of the border.

Spread across Niger and Kwara states around Kainji Dam, these two people groups are almost totally Muslim. The area has churches, but these are made up almost entirely of other tribes.

The Easter weekend marked an historic milestone for them. Thanks to Ross' dedication and God's provision they now have the Bible (70 percent), a dictionary, literacy primers, and the history of their area in their mother tongue. I was privileged to attend the dedication of these books at the Emir's palace in Kaiama. We were thankful to see God's Word appreciated even by Muslims, who gave speeches. The local government pledged to use the primers in the primary schools right away.

We live in a day in which smaller language groups are dying out. Up to 150,000 people speak these three languages. Hausa, the trade language spoken around us, is threatening to take over. Ross has given these people hope that their languages will survive. But more than that, they can talk to God in the language of their heart, and they can know the joy of being forgiven.

This is a key time to pray for these people groups. May the God who loves them and speaks their language send laborers to bring them into his family!

In June we organized a dinner at Murrumbeena Baptist church to celebrate the publication of the Bokobaru and Bisā Bibles. Seventy supporters of our work and thirty Indian friends attended. Everyone enjoyed the delicious curries made by the Indians. Our sons all contributed; Peter was MC, Andrew gave a PowerPoint presentation which included a video of the launching ceremonies, Paul sang a song he composed for the occasion, and Matthew reported on his trip to Nigeria and Benin with me.

PART 4

REAPING THE HARVEST

The Boys Launch Out

1996-2004

Matthew and Ros' wedding
Paul, Naomi with Hudson, Andrew, Ross, Neville,
Matt, Ros, Sal, Pete, with Noah and Joy in front

It was a real pleasure for Joy and me to see our boys developing over the years. Being active and fun-loving, there were times when they got involved in rascally behavior, but on the whole, they were responsible lads, and as they matured, they all had leadership roles. During these years they succeeded in their secondary school studies and the tertiary courses of their choice. They entered the workforce, chose their partners and got married. Each one has developed in his own way socially, musically and spiritually. As missionaries we were delighted to see them studying theology and serving Jesus in various ways, but we didn't pressure them in that direction. We had trained them early: "Start children off on the way they should go, and even when they are old they will not turn from it" (Proverbs 22:6).

Here is a brief summary of their lives during the following years. When Andrew turned twenty-one, he had a catered party for his friends in our back yard, after which he successfully finished his BA at Monash university. At Christmas he coordinated the teenage program at the Portland Family Mission and continued his Bachelor of Theology studies full time at Ridley College. He worked two days a week as a staff worker for the Australian Fellowship of Evangelical Students (AFES) at Monash and did two days a week at a factory while he finished his degree. He said that life had progressed a long way from those days when the family arguments were over Baba, Paul's monkey doll. I ended that saga by tossing the doll out the window at sixty mph somewhere in deepest Africa. Now each of the boys has his own daily commitments and new stresses. We thank God deeply for his faithfulness in making them his and keeping them.

At twenty-three Andrew finished the second year of his theology degree and celebrated the second anniversary of going out with his 'cute and clever friend' Naomi Palmer. Naomi completed her B.Sc. and moved on to do a post-graduate Social Work degree at Melbourne University. The following year Andrew was appointed to represent the work of SIM and SIMaid at universities, churches and schools. To be better informed he was given a three-week trip to India to see the work first hand. This was a real eye-opener for him, as he saw aid projects in action, interacted with Christians, and saw the vast need. On New Year's Eve he and Naomi were engaged.

Andrew left home at age twenty-four and lived at a Syndal Baptist church house. He was working for the church as the youth staff worker. In July he and Naomi were married at the Scotch College chapel. He finished his Theology degree and they celebrated with a holiday in Tasmania. When Andrew finished two years at Syndal and Naomi finished her Social Work degree they moved to Thornbury and Andrew worked for SIM two days a week and as associate pastor at Moonee Ponds Baptist Church. He also had a part time role in training pastors with Caleb ministries, and he went to Hyderabad in India for a few weeks as part of a team of instructors.

In 1999 Andrew & Naomi visited South Africa. From there, he took Naomi to where he went to school in Nigeria, to where he lived in Benin, and finally they spent a few days with me at Kaiama. On returning to Australia, he resigned as pastor of Moonee Ponds and worked full time with Caleb Ministries as training coordinator. He took seminars as far away as New Zealand and Hong Kong. They moved to Blackburn, and then Andrew took on a new consulting job at Medibank Private. They welcomed their first child, Noah, in December 2003 and the following year he started working as a Training Consultant. In 2013 Andrew and family went to Tanzania to serve with SIM for three years.

Andrew became chairman of the SIM Victoria State Council while Naomi worked part time in Family Therapy. Later Naomi was invited to join the SIM Council. They now have four children, Noah, Hudson, Mali and Reuben.

After secondary school Paul attended Box Hill TAFE where he completed a course in music performance. In the midyear break he participated in a music tour, playing trumpet with two black American gospel singers. Music was a big part of his life and at his 21st birthday party, guests came dressed as famous musicians. In 1993 he was the leader of a Christian band that played at various churches and gatherings. He did a Bachelor of Ministries at the Bible College of Victoria in 1995-97 and although this took most of his time, he also continued with his music ministry. He found his years at BCV encouraging and challenging. His faith grew and developed in many ways through new friendships, Bible study and practical ministries. He used to sing and share his testimony in various churches.

Paul went to Canada where he did a Masters in Christian Education at Regent College, Vancouver, majoring in creative ministries. He also did in-depth studies in Old Testament and Hebrew. He married at the age of twenty-three, and they had two daughters, but unfortunately after six years their marriage broke down irretrievably ending in divorce. This was a time of confusion and great distress for all the family. Paul stayed with me for some time and then he went overseas including a week in Morocco and a wedding in Switzerland with Matthew, and then they both hiked around Corsica for ten days.

In 2007 Paul moved to England to live and found work teaching RE full time at St Paul's Catholic School in Milton Keynes. The following year he was engaged to Anakatrina (Katy) Nenadovic. Katy has been a wonderful wife for Paul, and it was great that I could attend their wedding in UK in August on my way home from Nigeria. They came to Australia at the end of their honeymoon so that Katy could meet all the family, and especially Joy.

In 2010 they spent nine months in Argentina on a short-term mission project. Paul has launched into a promising new career. He wrote a book called 'Sharing God's Passion' on prophetic spirituality which was published by Paternoster. That was followed up by another book, 'Job's way through pain'. He did his PhD in theology at Durham University with the aim of becoming an Old Testament professor.

Paul and Katy and their two girls, Anasofia (Sofi) and Eden, moved to Brisbane, Australia in 2016, where Paul taught Old Testament and preaching classes at Trinity Theological College. In 2019 he was appointed principal.

Vuk and Lindsay Nenadovic, Katy, Paul and Ross

Matthew finished year twelve in 1994 and went on to do a Science course at Monash University where he made new friends at Christian Union. Each year at Christmas he was a leader at the Youth Dimension coffee shop at Port Fairy, and he helped lead Sunday School and a youth group at Murrumbeena Baptist. He bought a car as soon as he turned eighteen.

After his science degree, in which he majored in zoology and immunology, he did a TESL (Teaching English as a Second Language) course at Holmesglen TAFE. He went to Thailand on an Australian Baptist Missionary Society mission awareness trip for three weeks, and on his return, he did a graduate diploma in Christian Studies at the Bible College of Victoria. In the following year he was a student representative, and he completed his Master of Arts.

Then he went on a world trip for nearly eight months through Canada, US, Europe, Turkey, Nepal and India. He enjoyed seeing the wider world, reflecting on things, and he developed an interest in exploring alternative ways of running church. He worked for a while as notetaker for disabled tertiary students and teaching interns at Youth Dimension. Finally, he did a Diploma of Education at Melbourne University and started his teaching career at Altona Secondary College. After twelve months there, he found that Mt Evelyn Christian school was more his style.

Matthew was a leader in a church planting venture in Croydon, and it was there at the Eastern Hills Community Church that he met Roslyn Clarke. They were married at Warrandyte just before his 30th birthday. They settled down in their home in Mitcham. Ros had studied law, and she worked for Tear Australia, a Christian aid agency. Her father, Dr Graeme Clark, pioneered the cochlear implant for severe to profound deafness, the first major advance in helping deaf children and adults communicate in a world of sound.

Ros gave birth to Tessa in 2008 and sadly their second child, Solomon, was stillborn at twenty weeks. A funeral service was held for him. Matt also taught at Donvale Christian School, but then he launched into a pastoral career at Northern Community Church of Christ in Preston. In 2019 he moved to Crossway Baptist Church in Burwood, where he leads one of their community out-reach programs.

When youngest son Peter finished year ten, he went on his first Coffee Shop at Rosebud. Then he started his VCE with mainly business subjects. He was in the diving team and his guitar lessons were coming along well. He played guitar at Murrumbeena Baptist, joined a band with a few friends from school, played in the Show Band in his last year at Scotch, and coordinated the music at coffee shop. He was baptized at Murrumbeena to affirm his faith in Jesus and his willingness to live for him.

After VCE, he started a Commerce/Education double degree at Deacon University which was only ten minutes from home. It was a big year with university studies, first year of driving, and first year with girlfriend Sallie. He worked part-time teaching guitar and part-time in Bob Killick's chemical factory where the other boys had worked. He also led the youth group at Murrumbeena and a coffee shop at Barham. After completing two years of his degrees, Peter deferred for a year, working at a scrap-metal factory for six months and travelling overseas with a friend for five months. That trip included two weeks of Spartan conditions with me in Nigeria and six weeks with Paul in Canada. He also visited South Africa, USA and New Zealand. Pete had his 21st birthday in February 2000 and celebrated with a party for one-hundred guests under marquees in the backyard. Pete's antics and achievements were highlighted.

After qualifying as a secondary teacher and marketer, he worked temporarily at Holden as a sales representative before taking up a full-time job as an internal sales manager at Corporate Express.

Pete and Sallie were married in February 2003 and lived at Hughesdale. Peter moved to sales manager in the furniture department, while Sallie finished her Arts degree in Public Relations. From Hughesdale they moved to Brighton, and then they moved to Lakes Entrance where Sallie worked in the family ice-cream business while Pete continued as a salesman.

From there they moved to Warragul, where they bought a house, and Peter did a Graduate Diploma in Evaluations while doing a related property valuer job for two years. Sallie finished her marketing office role at Mt Baw Baw, and William Ross (Billy) was born, followed later by his sister Eve and brother Max.

Ross with grandchildren (2013)

Indian student work

1997-2010

Indian Bible study group

In 1997 I was preaching at the church we planted in Ormond, when I noticed three Indian students in the congregation. Over coffee one of them named Steven told me that both his grandfathers were pastors, so I asked him what he was doing for the Lord. He said: "Nothing!" The result of that conversation was that I started doing a weekly Bible study with him. Soon, other Indian students joined us and an Indian Bible study group was formed that lasted for seven years. Twenty years later I am still in touch with Steven, his wife and two children, and about thirty of his relatives, and hundreds of other Indians. Steven's brother and numerous cousins also migrated to Melbourne, and many of them were in my Bible study group, which helped them develop their spiritual lives. At one stage there were thirty students in the group and we had two meetings a week.

Some of the students were strong Christians while others were from traditional denominations and didn't really know the Lord yet. Most of them were from Christian families where church attendance was important. I devised a questionnaire which I asked newcomers to fill in. That information gave me a good idea where each one stood spiritually. It was important to guide those who were nominal believers into a meaningful relationship with Christ. Some of them lived with Hindu friends and there was always the danger of them getting seduced by the world and caught up in a life of drinking and nightclubs. The Bible study group had a stabilizing influence on them.

Most of the Indians I know are from the Indian States of Andhra Pradesh and Telangana, where they all speak Telugu. I never learnt Telugu because I had too many African languages going around in my head. I didn't realize at that time that the friendships would go on for decades. There is another group in Melbourne called the Melbourne Telugu Christian Fellowship (MTCF). They meet monthly and the emphasis is on Telugu families, but students are also welcome and encouraged to press on in their Christian lives. Christian fellowship is so important, and this isn't always provided by the church, especially those where people just attend services and don't get involved in serving God or meeting in smaller groups. A small group of 12-15 people is an ideal environment for young people to learn how to walk in the Spirit. They become accountable to each other, and they can share their doubts and struggles during the prayer times. They learn to know what God's will is and respond as they are encouraged to do it.

Our meetings lasted 2-3 hours. From my experience with Indian Christians, I found that they were more spiritually active than their Aussie counterparts. Indian pastors are more demanding that their young people toe the line, whereas Australians shun rules and tradition. Our meetings started with half an hour of praise. Musicians weren't always available, but as we progressed, song leaders and musicians developed their skills. The Bible study and discussion would go for at least forty minutes, and then there was a time of prayer. Everyone had the chance to share their worries and pray for each other. And after that was the meal – the delicious Indian curries prepared by the host or other members.

In 2001 I made two trips to India on my way to West Africa. On the first trip, I was met at Hyderabad airport by six of my friends who had either returned to India or were there temporarily. They had a minibus and we went around visiting their families and families of my student friends back in Melbourne. Everywhere I went there was wonderful hospitality. Most families were Christian and inevitably they would ask me to bring them a message and pray for them. On some occasions they gathered relatives and friends together. I visited fifteen homes. Then there was a young man named Emmanuel with whom I had been corresponding for some time. He lived at Kazipet, about 80 km north of Hyderabad, so we travelled up there and stayed the night with his family. The colors of India are amazing. Even on country roads, brightly colored temples and other decorated buildings are commonplace. Swarms of people everywhere and chaotic traffic without rules were my early impressions.

I became interested in the Banjara people and did a lot of research into their situation. They are a gypsy type people who exist in most Indian States. The New Testament had been translated into Banjara (also known as Lambadi) in Telangana and then Banjaras in other

States were adapting it to their dialect. The Andhra Pradesh version had at least 25% Telugu words and I was concerned that this was being done in an amateurish way and saw the need for a proper language survey to be done among all the Banjaras of India. I thought this was something I could get involved in when my work in Nigeria finished.

There were SIL related people in Nasik in Maharashtra State who were well trained in doing language surveys, but there had been some misunderstanding between them and the Banjaras. I did a lot of research and organizing on the internet, getting in touch with many people who had an interest in the Banjara. Later in 2001 I went back to India, visited Nasik and accompanied some of their personal to Hyderabad where I had organized a conference with Banjara leaders. The two sides discussed the issue and came to an agreement about doing a good Banjara language survey and using that as a basis for future Banjara translations. In the end they looked at me and said: "What role will you play?" I had noticed that they had people qualified to do everything, including the Scripture adaptation program that I thought I would help them with. So, I gracefully bowed out. Lambadi population estimates range up to forty million. Each translation has to be done in the Script of the Indian State in which they live, and many are now in progress.

In 2003 I went to Bangaluru (Bangalore) to visit a Manipuri young man named Tomchou whom I had led to the Lord on the internet. He started calling himself Tom Jones. In 2007 I went to Hyderabad again and a friend Calvin Vemavarapu accompanied me to Delhi and a hill station in the Himalayan foothills called Shimla, which was very interesting. After that I travelled with another friend, James Chedalavada, to his hometown of Bhimavaram, where we spent a few days looking around and I preached to a gathering in his home and at a church in a town nearby.

About 100 people passed through the Ormond Bible study group, and then in 2004 James asked me to start a group at his flat in Footscray. It was a long way from Glen Waverley, but I knew that the Western suburbs of Melbourne had fewer Christians than the east, and I was keen to make a contribution over there. James lived with four Hindus whom we hoped would join the group, but they didn't, and we had to meet in his bedroom. The group remained small, but after some time we moved to the flat of James Rapaka in Essendon, where six Christian students lived. The group thrived in that location for a couple of years and again many young students were encouraged and helped to grow in their spiritual lives. It was also training for many of them as they got involved in hospitality, leading the singing, leading the prayer time, and leading a Bible study. When that venue was no longer available, we moved to Flemington for some months and then out to Niddrie.

Joy had moved into hostel care at Cumberland View in Wheelers Hill in January 2006. The boys had left home and being alone in the house, I took in several Indian boarders including James Chedalavada who matured spiritually and became a leader of the large Essendon Bible study group.

After Joy's passing in 2009, I bought a large two-story house in Braybrook, near Footscray, only seven miles from the city. I took in a dozen Indian student boarders, and Braybrook became the center for our Bible study group, although another group continued at Essendon. I continued living in the east but spent the weekends with my boarders at Braybrook. I was helping them to have cheap board in a Christian environment, in a house which had plenty of room. They each paid $100 a week for food and lodgings which included all bills – electricity, gas, water, phone, internet, and Foxtel. Two people were rostered for cooking each night and two for cleaning the kitchen and dining area. Each person had another job cleaning a bedroom, bathroom, lounge, putting out rubbish, etc. The system worked pretty well for eighteen months but then I received a letter from the local council saying that it had come to their notice that my house was being used as a boarding house and was not registered for that purpose. Inspectors came out and said that because of the size of the house, a sprinkling system would have to be installed. The cost of doing that was prohibitive and I also had had other problems. There was not that sense of unity that I expected from my Christian tenants, and some of them were getting lax in paying their rent. There was also a new project on the horizon in Nigeria, so I decided to close down. The house was sold a couple of months later with a small profit, and I paid back my loan to the bank.

Each year we had a couple of outreach meetings at Easter and Christmas, so that we could explain the meaning of these festivals to Hindu and Muslim guests who were invited. We usually had over 100 attending and as usual, everyone was fed with Indian curries. Another activity was the picnic. It was good just to have a relaxing time together and to see the sights around Melbourne. We climbed the rocky tors at Hanging Rock, explored the goldfields at Ballarat, drove down the beautiful Great Ocean Road to the Twelve Apostles, visited the penguins at Phillip Island and the kangaroos on the Mornington Peninsula, dared to ski the slopes of Mt Bulla and Mt Baw Baw and climbed challenging slopes in the Grampians and the Cathedral Ranges.

In 2007 FUESIA was born. FUESIA stands for Friends of UESI Australia, and UESI stands for Union of Evangelical Students in India, a group that disciples students in Indian universities (like AFES in Australia). FUESIA started simultaneously in several Australian States, but the committee in Melbourne led by Emmanuel Ravuri consisted mainly of members of the Ormond and Essendon Bible study groups. I was happy to amalgamate my groups with FUESIA because it gave sustainability to the ministry I had started. I wouldn't be doing it forever, and now there were others who could carry on the vision. FUESIA continues to promote fellowship among Indian students, organize outreach to non-Christians, and conduct camps and inspirational meetings.

The number of Indian students dried up considerably in 2010. There were three reasons for this. There had many student bashings in Melbourne, especially of Indian students, and so parents back in India were reluctant to send their children there. Secondly, immigration laws had tightened up, making it harder for students to get their permanent residency. Finally, the strong Australian dollar at that time made it more expensive for Indian students to come to Australia. So, after fourteen years my Bible study work came to an end.

However, the Indian groups continue and now there are more Indian students than ever. There are several Bible-study groups in the east that have developed from the original group in Ormond. And the western suburbs group still meets monthly. Most of the original students now have stable jobs, are married, have bought houses, have borne children and are serving the Lord in various capacities.

Many of my friends are Indians. I spent fourteen years fellowshipping with them and got to know a few hundred of them. Sometimes I go to their homes for meals or am asked to give a devotional message at a birthday party. I am the adopted grandfather of one large family group regularly joining them in their celebrations. I still play tennis with students I taught how to play, but I can't seem to beat them for very long. Since Joy's passing, I have had Indian boarders living with me in Wheelers Hill. It is good to have their company. They are rostered to do the cooking and cleaning.

In October 2010 I celebrated my 70th birthday at Wheelers Hill with 100 guests, including all the family and 60 Indians. I thanked God for bringing me that far with good health and energy and vowed to continue to serve him as long as he gave me the strength and enthusiasm. 75 mm of rain on that day was symbolic of his showers of blessing in my life over the years.

Joy's Painful Journey

2002-2009

**Joy and baby Tessa, three months
before she went to be with the Lord**

From 2002 on, Joy was increasingly confined to a wheelchair. She had pain, but more significantly she became completely disabled. I took over all the household duties and everywhere we went, I wheeled her in the wheelchair. The rheumatoid arthritis was affecting every joint in her body. Initially she had problems with her hands and feet, but this had spread to knees, hips, shoulders and elbows. She had a dozen operations. Even her jaw joints were affected by arthritis and then part of her jaw started dying, due to a drug she was taking. She used to suffer from asthma in the early years of our marriage, but when the arthritis started, the asthma retreated. But in her final years the breathing problems returned.

The year 2002 was perhaps the most difficult year for Joy, and that had followed seventeen years of progressive arthritis. Many operations on her joints had already weakened her body. In February her right ankle was fused to reduce the pain. That necessitated many weeks of sitting still and being fully cared for. She was in a wheelchair for a month and then walked a little with the plaster for a month. It was two weeks to go before the plaster came off, when the unthinkable happened. Joy related the incident:

> We were leaving our good friends the Greenwoods' home after a visit, when I tripped on the join between the carpet and the tiles and fell heavily on the tiles breaking my left femur just above the artificial knee. The pain was excruciating.

She was rushed off to Epworth in an ambulance, and thanks to God, there was a bed available. After the operation she had another six weeks without walking. Then she went into rehabilitation to learn to walk again on two repaired legs after four months of sitting.

Joy was able to walk in the house with a frame, but seven months after the operation the doctor found there was no healing in her leg, and she had to have a bone graft in November. She was never able to walk well after that.

I drove her to physiotherapy and hydrotherapy twice a week. She had so many painful areas. The fused ankle continued to give pain, as did her left shoulder, her neck and her jaw. In 2004 the pain in her neck continued and we discovered that the she had an infection in her lower jaw as a side effect of an arthritic drug she had taken for many years. In September she celebrated her sixtieth birthday with forty guests at our home, but she was very fragile and teary.

In November she had another hip replacement at Epworth. Then at the age of ninety, her dear Mum went into Karana nursing home with Alzheimer's disease.

By 2005 I was finding the constant caring a burden. It involved dressing Joy, helping her getting in and out of bed, helping with toileting and eating, and lifting the wheelchair in and out of the car many times a week when we went out for doctor's appointments, visiting parents, church, and drives to the shopping center, park or beach. I loved my wife and wanted to help her as much as I could, but she was frustrated and struggling with her physical weakness and pain and feeling vulnerable. It seemed that I was the only one she could blame. She didn't want me to leave her for more than a few hours at a time and became very critical of the Indian ministry I was doing in the western suburbs. She would constantly question the sincerity of my motives.

When I was due to return to Benin in January 2006, I told Joy that she really needed to be in respite care while I was away. It was hard to get carers coming to the house, and I felt that she needed full-time supervision. She reluctantly agreed to go into Cumberland View Hostel for respite care for six weeks while I was away. This was a hard decision, but her condition was such that it wasn't wise or practical for her to be alone, even for a few hours of time.

She found it better than she had thought. On my return, as she was feeling more positive about the place, and I felt she was better off there, she was given a permanent place. One of her concerns was that she was only in her early sixties whereas the average age of people in the hostel was well into the eighties. Over time Joy became unhappy with the situation and found it a huge emotional upheaval.

She felt lonely and missed our family home a lot. She accused me of rejecting her in preference for some Indian friends as boarders I had taken in. She talked about getting out and living on her own, but I knew that that was not an option. Some people were critical of my decision, but my family and close friends understood the situation more intimately.

She didn't go to the dining room or mix with the other residents much, but she did have a great time with the carers. They seemed to migrate to her because she had an active mind, and she always had a sympathetic ear to listen to people with their problems.

In August Joy was rushed to hospital with a dislocated hip which stabilized. We had a great day at Matt's wedding in January. Although in a wheelchair, she didn't want to look dowdy, so she bought a bright red dress for the occasion and some ladies at the hostel made her up beautifully. But in February 2007 after several hip dislocations she had to have a cap put on it. She was in hospital for two weeks and following the anesthetic she had a torrid time with breathing problems, including some days in intensive care. From then on, she had an oxygen unit in her room at Cumberland View.

The carer's job is a difficult one. Joy appreciated all I did for her, but she was frustrated by the fact that she couldn't do anything, whereas I was always fit and well and into so many things. My family members and friends thought I was doing a great job looking after Joy, but Joy's confidants were hearing another story and I soon had my pastor and two friends meeting regularly with me to give guidance and encouragement. They encouraged me to retire from SIM in July 2008, which I did, so that I was free to spend more time with Joy. But her days were drawing to an end.

The Glen Waverley home was sold in early 2008, and Joy and I looked for another home closer to her hostel. It was obvious to many that she would always need professional care, but Joy thought she would be independent again one day. We chose a lovely home with a view of the hills in Wheelers Hill, but Joy was only able to spend some afternoons there. I moved into the new house in August and took Joy there a few times, but I knew that she would never be able to live there. She had had no health crises for fifteen months, but she had a lot of chronic problems related to her arthritis, bronchitis, damaged lungs and blood pressure.

August 14th was the beginning of the end for Joy when she came down with pneumonia. She was in hospital for twelve days, including two days in intensive care. Three weeks out of hospital and she had to go back again with persistent pneumonia. Her lung capacity was small and her resistance low due to her faulty immune system. Her throat often felt restricted and her lower legs had been badly swollen for some time.

She coped alright until January. In the last week of her life she wasn't feeling at all well and wondered if she should be in hospital. We called the doctor twice, but it wasn't until she woke up in a semi coma that they took her to hospital. The boys and I remained by her bedside for twenty-four hours, but she didn't regain consciousness. Joy was called home to be with the Lord on January 10th, 2009, aged sixty-four.

The funeral at Syndal Baptist church was a triumphant occasion with several hundred people present. Paul came home from London, and all the boys gave a eulogy, a poem or a song. We all miss her vibrant personality and there was a feeling of loneliness for me after thirty-seven years of marriage. We had always shared with each other everything going on in our lives.

When the second edition of the Boko Bible was dedicated in July 2010, the daily devotional book called Daily Light, which was translated into Boko, was launched in her memory. In the frontispiece it said:

> She served the Lord wholeheartedly, she cared for the sick daily, she taught God's word to women and children and bore four children. This book is in memory of her, so that we don't forget the love she had for everyone or the zeal she had in spreading the good news in the Boko area.

This is the eulogy that Paul composed and read:

A Mother's strength

You came into the world surrounded by grief already
A difficult way to start
But your parents gave you a name against the odds
A name to pave the way for what would come
Sharing your faith in God with people around the world
Strengthening the weak by inviting them into your heart
Accepting whoever came your way with a kind smile
Laughing with your sons, helping us believe in ourselves
Your body has been frail for as long as I can remember
But your spirit strong – and compassionate
You've listened when others have turned away
Your presence and love have been as reliable as a mountain
When I have felt alone and misunderstood
And you have been like this for so many

I do not doubt that at some unknown time in the future
You will stand surrounded
By people you have touched with the hands of Christ
A multitude touched by God-in-you
And your body will be renewed – just like you've always wanted
Your hands will hold other hands – tightly
And they will physically feel what has made you strong
The Spirit of our earth's Maker within you
For eternity you will continue to be strong
And you will keep bringing goodness into the lives of others
For that is who you are – your name is Joy

In retirement I kept in regular touch with my four boys and my grandchildren. I thank God that they are all doing well and following Jesus while living in a secular society that has largely turned their back on God and his standards.

Joy's parents both outlived their only daughter. Her mother Bessie died in 2012 and her father, the Rev Neville Horn, in 2013. They both died at the age of ninety-seven. They were well cared for at Karana, the Baptist nursing home in Kew. They were wonderful parents-in-law to me, and they always took a great interest in our family and our ministry. When in Australia, I visited them there at Karana every week until the end.

Boko Bible Revision

---◆---

2005–2010

Greeting local dignitaries at the Boko Bible launch

With the Bokobaru and Bisã adaptations finished in Nigeria, I again turned my attention to the Boko church in Benin Republic. There were only a few hundred Boko Bibles left and I felt that we should revise it before doing a reprint. The translation was good, we didn't need to change the way it was expressed, but there were two features that I wanted to improve; the marking of tone, and the joining together of compound words. Then there was the dictionary. While working in Nigeria I had published a Boko-English dictionary, and the Boko people in Benin saw it and requested a Boko-French dictionary, French being the national language of Benin and the language of school education.

When the Boko Bible was published in 1992, I didn't have a very good grasp of the complicated tone system in the Boko language. I learnt a lot when I did my PhD. Every syllable of every word has its own tone. That is called lexical tone. On top of that there is grammatical tone which affects all verbs and pronouns and sometimes nouns as well. If you mark all the tone, the script becomes too messy and hard to read, so you have to work out a system where you only mark enough tone to avoid ambiguities. We did our best for the first edition of the Bible, but sometimes readers got confused and didn't know whether they should read a word with high, mid or low tone. When I did my PhD research, I cracked all the tone mysteries of the Boko language and I was then able to formulate a more practical tone marking system.

Joining words together was a different matter. Let me explain it a little. In Boko the Direct Object comes before the verb, so they say, I milk drank, rather than, I drank milk. There are some verbs that have a very broad meaning, but when compounded with a Direct Object, the meaning is clear. For example, 'mouth-tie' means 'to fast'. In the past we wrote 'mouth' and 'tie' separately, but my Boko translation team said that they don't think of fasting as tying the mouth, but the combination of those words together. Instead of 'le ye' they wanted to write 'leye'. They convinced me, and I decided to join them. But grammar has rules, and so I had to make a rule when a Direct Object should be joined to the verb and when it should remain separate. My conclusion was that when the Direct Object was a short noun of one or two syllables, and in the context, it had a general sense and was unmodified, it should be joined to the verb. This worked well, but it meant that over one thousand Boko compound verbs had to be joined.

Just these two modifications to tone and compound verbs meant countless changes to the Boko Bible. John 3:16 had eleven changes! The result is an easier text to read. It took several years to accomplish, but at the same time we were working on the Boko-French-English dictionary. Ten-thousand-word dictionaries in small languages are rare, but I love a challenge. I had already published a seven-thousand-word dictionary in Boko-English, and when I found that Levi's son Isaac could help me with the French meanings, I knew that we could produce something good for the Benin Boko. The dictionary was embellished with 665 scientific names (in Latin) of fauna and flora. I bought a book on the internet which described hundreds of trees of the sub-Saharan savannah where the Boko live. It had several colored illustrations for each tree and Levi, who has an encyclopedic knowledge of the trees in the Boko bush, had a wonderful time matching 240 of them with their Boko names. He also has an excellent knowledge of the animals, birds, reptiles and insects in the area. The-586-page dictionary was published by Lincom Europa and made available to linguists and universities around the world, just as the PhD thesis and the other dictionaries had been.

One day I was eating with Levi at his home village of Saonzi. "It's a long time since we had chicken," I queried. Levi explained that most chickens had died in an outbreak of chicken cholera. I felt an urge to help the Bokos in their poverty. Not only was there a shortage of meat, there was no training program or capital available for people to launch into something new. In addition, the average Christian family had five children and educating them only added to their struggle. After thinking and praying about this situation, I came to hear about DEDRAS, an NGO who specialized in sustainable development. They are an arm of the SIM related UEEB church in Benin. I wanted them to help me alleviate the

Boko poverty. I thought I could raise $20-30,000 a year for two years and DEDRAS could do the practical work through their trained agricultural and veterinary staff. I also wanted them to help support Boko students in the final years of secondary school and on into tertiary level.

A date was arranged for me to meet with the director of DEDRAS. I walked away from our meeting having been talked into a four-year project with a AU$70,000 annual budget. This was a challenge! I was nervous about it, but felt it was God's will. DEDRAS wrote up their proposal and I presented it to SIMaid, SIM Australia's tax-deductible aid agency. The project was accepted and advertised in my regular newsletter and by SIMaid. Over the four-year period (2007-2010) $250,000 was given by Australian Christians.

The project had six components:

- technical support and micro-lending for eighty crop farmers each year
- training and loans for eighty chicken/animal breeders
- training in small business and loans for sixty women
- access to cheap drugs and mosquito nets
- train two nurses at university level in Niamey
- financial help for fifty students living away from home

The program was geared to be sustainable; loans being paid back with ten-percent interest. When the initial four years of the project were finished, loans and training continued to be given in an ongoing program. Here is a testimony written for me by Makido Simeon, one of the farmers:

> I prepared one hectare of maize. Thanks to the loan, I have fertilizer and seed. I made up the balance with my own money. Since I have a pair of oxen, I carried out the ploughing myself. I am very happy with Ross's support, because he enables me to have pride and dignity. I hope to harvest fifty sacks of maize,

approximately 5.6 tons. I will then be the happiest
man in Segbana. My field is clean, thanks to the loan.

In January 2008 we organized a literacy seminar at Segbana. On
the mayor's authority delegates were invited from every Boko village.
About eighty people came and the mayor opened proceedings, followed
by speeches from the president of the Boko language commission and
me. I outlined my thirty-nine years of work among the Boko and my
leading role in Boko literacy and literature production. Most of the
participants were Muslim and they were lamenting the fact that the
government literacy program had died, while the church program
had been very successful. Over all those years the leaders of the
government program had not sincerely cooperated with us, as many
Muslims felt uneasy about using literature produced by Christians.

When we broke into four groups to discuss different challenges,
I led the group which discussed the question: "How to continue the
production of Boko literacy and teaching materials?" The first man
who spoke, a literacy coordinator, rose and said: "The only solution is
to put it all in the hands of the church." Wow! I was excited. No one
objected. They also passed a resolution that the literature we produce
for general use should have the government imprimatur on it, so that
everyone would know that it is acceptable. A committee was elected
with Pastor Levi as president.

The dedication of the second edition of the Boko Bible was held
at Segbana on July 24th, 2010 and attended by six to seven-hundred
people. Also dedicated was the Boko-French-English dictionary and
the daily devotional book "Daily Light" which was translated into
Boko with a frontispiece in memory of Joy. 20,000 Boko booklets
were printed altogether by the "Empowering the Boko" project,
including a history of Borgu and a collection of 417 Boko proverbs.
The consignment of Bibles from China had been held up at the port.
We were kept in suspense for several weeks and finally had to go
ahead with the launching with only one copy of Daily Light and the
Bible on hand. A disappointment for me, but the locals didn't seem
to mind, as there was great interest in the dictionary and booklets.

Church and mission leaders travelled 250 km from Parakou over rainy-season affected roads as did several journalists and a TV team. A traditional "stick" dance was performed by a dozen Boko men, hitting wooden staffs simultaneously as they pranced around and sometimes somersaulted on the ground. The mayor of Segbana, a Muslim, gave a rousing speech in which he praised the work of the Boko translation team in saving their ethnic group from extinction and making the Boko language known worldwide. He even praised the pastors for their valuable work.

After forty years of involvement with the Boko people of Benin Republic, I felt that my contribution was complete. God had called me to be his representative among this people group, to translate the Bible, preach the gospel and develop the Boko church. To make this effectively happen, I had also been involved in literacy, medical work and agricultural work to alleviate their poverty. In July 2011 the mayor, Boko Language Commission personnel and the Segbana FM radio station personnel organized a small gathering of Boko leaders to decorate me and my co-worker Levi for the work we had done. After many speeches they presented us with African robes and they gave me a painting which depicted Boko women welcoming me and presenting me with calabashes full of shea nuts. It had the inscription: "The Boko are honoring you."

The Boko church is now well developed with churches in thirty-five towns and villages and over 3,500 Christians. They have their own Bible school on two hectares of land, their own radio programs which are broadcast on FM radio several times a week, their own Bible and dictionary and about thirty smaller booklets written in Boko. They have two Christian bookshops and several Christian clinics. The church has an annual conference, and the women and youth and children all have their own annual camps with many hundreds attending.

70th birthday celebration (2010)
Sal, Pete, Naomi, Ros, Matt with Tessa,
then in front Katy with Billy, Paul, Noah,
Andrew with Mali, Ross with Hudson

WHAT ABOUT KYANGA AND SHANGA?

2010 -2017

Chatting with Kyanga mullahs in Niger Republic

I found that life's happiness comes from a walk with the living God; not from drinking, travelling, or accumulating stuff. Pursuit of Christlikeness is far richer than being a film buff. Our Australian culture has lost many of the great Christian values that my African and Indian friends are more likely to embrace. For example, acknowledging Christ when entertaining friends at each other's homes, by including a devotional time or a time of praise or prayer, should be commonplace, but this is rarely done in our culture.

I enjoy watching golf, tennis and football on TV when I need to relax, but I can't be bothered with most films, soap operas, videos, and novels. M-rated movies are out. "Or what fellowship can light have with darkness? What harmony is there between Christ and Belial?" (2 Corinthians 6:14-15).

Spending time in Bible reading and prayer is never a waste of time. Telling God about your day's activities often results in bright ideas and a change of plans. Jesus "goes on ahead of them, and his sheep follow him because they know his voice" (John 10:4).

Nine months after retiring from SIM and three months after Joy went to be with the Lord, I wrote to a German historiographer, named Richard Kuba, whom I had met a few times in Nigeria. He had written a paper about Borgu and Levi requested that I email him and ask him for a copy of the paper. After making my request, I told him that I had retired from SIM, that my wife had passed away, and that I had finished revising all the Boko literature. I wrote: "I think I'm going to get bored now. Do you have any suggestions?" His emailed reply came back the same day. "What about Kyanga and Shanga?" he said. I immediately identified with his suggestion; it was a message from the Great Shepherd of the sheep. He also told me that a German linguist, Professor Henning Schreiber was interested in these languages and we might do something together.

Kyanga and Shanga are two small endangered languages in Nigeria, closely related to Boko and not too far from the Boko area. Nobody knew the exact situation of these two tribes and when I wrote to Henning expressing my interest in doing some work on these languages, he replied to me: "I am convinced that you are the only person in our academic field who has reliable information on these languages and we could not apply for any funding without your assistance." So together we applied for funding from a German foundation which funds the documentation of endangered languages. Our application was not accepted.

In June 2010 I was going to Segbana for the launching of the second edition of the Boko Bible and other literature, so I phoned Levi and told him that we had a new adventure ahead; to go and investigate the Kyanga and Shanga in Nigeria, take down some vocabulary, take photos, and record some stories with a Roland audio recorder.

The Kyanga area is only sixty miles north of Segbana, so we took off on his motorbike with three bags including computer and recording equipment. That was our transport for the next five weeks. We didn't know of anybody in the area, which is entirely Muslim, except that there was one church at Lolo and a Nigerian missionary named Ezra at Tungan Bage. The first night we went to Illo and greeted the Emir whom we had met eighteen years before when doing an earlier language survey. When we asked for accommodation at the government guest house, he said we could stay there for one night.

Next day we arrived in Lolo and found the pastor of the Yoruba Baptist Church and asked if we could stay at his house while we did some research on the Kyanga language. We ended up staying with him for three weeks. We slept on the verandah, preached at his church one Sunday, and used his generator at night to work on the computer and recharge the battery. There is no electricity in this area and there are very few people who speak English. Levi was fluent in Hausa, which is the lingua franca of the area; I couldn't have done this work without him. Each day we went to a Kyanga village and worked with different people who were very cooperative. We discovered that there were over two hundred thousand Kyanga people in Nigeria, Niger and Benin, but only twenty thousand who could still speak their own language. The rest of them had assimilated to the Hausa language. The Kyanga speakers lived in the five villages we were visiting. The weather was hot, the food average, and I had a heat rash on my chest, a sunburnt nose, and the occasional bout of diarrhea. I asked myself whether at sixty-nine, I was getting too old for this!

We crossed the mighty Niger River in a canoe and travelled thirty miles to Kyangakwai, which is the main Kyanga center. We gained a lot of information there, and an official letter of support from the secretary of the Kyanga Cultural Community. We were moving about in Kebbi State, one of the Nigerian states that has Sharia law, so it was always good to have letters of support from people in authority.

When visiting any tribal area, an audience with the local king at his palace is a courtesy one must not forget. On this occasion I was visiting the chief of all the Kyanga people. The Kyanga are predominantly Muslim and a Kyanga historian had been called from Niger Republic to come and share his knowledge with us. The king's entourage and other Africans were all seated on the floor, but I was given an armchair and sat next to the king. It hadn't rained for forty days, and the local farmers were very concerned and had been carrying out some rituals to make it rain. Our host, a Yoruba missionary named Jeremiah, Levi and I asked if we could pray in the name of Jesus for rain. The king agreed, and we each prayed in our respective languages. The next morning at five a.m. the heavens opened, and rain fell for seven hours. When leaving the next day, we stopped at the palace to say goodbye to the king. The last words we heard him say were to a woman standing nearby: "The Christians prayed for rain yesterday."

We travelled one-hundred miles to the Shanga area, which was a different story. The Muslim authorities were suspicious of us and sent us another one-hundred miles to Birnin Kebbi, the State capital, to get an authorization from the State Commissioner. That took two days.

At the palace of the Kyanga king

We sensed that the Lord was with us. On our return, when we entered the large town of Koko, we didn't know where to find the ECWA church, where we hoped to stay the night. As we were driving along the main road, Levi said: "Let's go into this household and ask." We asked a girl if she knew where the ECWA church was, and she replied that an elder of that church lived right there in that household! He took us to the ECWA pastor and we were welcomed to stay there for the night. We found that this pastor was an agriculturalist, and that he had visited all the villages in the Shanga area. He was able to tell us the ethnic makeup of all the villages and the precise villages where we would find Shanga speakers. We discovered that there were about twenty thousand Shanga people, with less than five-thousand still speaking the Shanga language. There was only one known Christian Shanga, a widow who had been married to a pastor. There was no Christian work being done there.

Next day we went to Sakace, the main Shanga-speaking town. We greeted the chief and showed him the authorization given by the Commissioner in Birnin Kebbi. However, he did not accept it and said that we would have to go to another town and get permission there. I suspected that he had had a phone call from the local government who had a reputation for not allowing any churches to be built in their villages, telling him not to cooperate with us.

With dejected faces, Levi and I were walking back to our motorbike on the edge of town, when a man approached us and asked what we wanted to do there. I explained that we were researching the Shanga language and wanted to take down one hundred words or so, as they were pronounced in his town. He said he was a councillor in the town and that the chief was a stubborn man. The chief wasn't an ethnic Shanga and so didn't care about this research, it wasn't his language. Our new friend told us to follow him and he would help us to do what we wanted.

He took us behind a mosque and brought a chair for me and soon there was a crowd of people around us. We spent an hour eliciting Shanga vocabulary and writing it down carefully in an exercise book. The chief sent messengers a couple of times to tell the councilor not to help us, but they were ignored.

That night we travelled twelve miles to the town of Yauri and stayed a few nights with the pastor of a church there who was happy to accommodate us. Then we travelled to a Shanga village on the south side of the Niger River, called Kawama. It was less Islamized than the other villages. Conditions were difficult as we traversed the Niger River twice in a small canoe. Once my computer bag fell into the water, but I was able to retrieve it before the water seeped through the zip to the computer. The chief was very friendly, and we got our wordlist done without any trouble.

Eliciting Shanga vocabulary

When leaving the Shanga area, we decided to return by a different route, and we planned to stay at the only church in that area, on the south side of the Niger River. The village was called Shabanda. We left a bit too late in the afternoon and we had to travel twenty-five miles further than expected. After crossing the Niger in a canoe with the motorbike, we started travelling on a sometimes slippery, and at other times sandy path. Levi was driving, I was on the back with our bags. Darkness had fallen, and then the headlight globe went out on this track that we hadn't travelled on before. Sitting behind Levi, I shone the torch on the track as he maneuvered between the slippery muddy patches and the holes causes by erosion. At 8:30 p.m. we came to a small tributary of the Niger that we couldn't cross. Then in the light of the moon we saw a canoeist gliding silently over the water from the other side. He took us across for a pittance, and then we travelled again by torchlight until we bought another headlight globe in the next village. We arrived at Shabanda at 9 p.m. and were warmly welcomed by the Christians there. One man, named Haruna, killed a rabbit for our dinner and the pastor gave us a nice place to sleep. Such is the hospitality of very poor people in remote villages. Next morning, I walked around the village with a big crowd of children following. They hadn't seen a white man before.

During this trip we discovered information that nobody had recorded before about the numbers and location of people who spoke Kyanga and Shanga. We took down hundreds of Kyanga and Shanga words and recorded ninety minutes of stories on the little Roland Edirol recorder.

Dying languages need to be documented and the Kyanga and Shanga people need the Lord. Our funding application took six months to process and wasn't successful, but I had already decided that I would do some Bible translation into these languages, and Levi and I had already made two trips to the area, one in June 2010 and the other in January 2011. Several Christians friends were funding the trips.

While there in January we attended a Kyanga cultural festival, where amongst the entertainment were two men wrestling with live hyenas which were muzzled. I was given the opportunity to speak about my research and I handed out copies of my current research to various leaders who were appreciative of what I was doing. Dictionaries and grammars were started and in June 2011 we distributed copies of booklets I had translated in their villages; a book of animal pictures with their names in Kyanga or Shanga, a counting book, a reading primer and the book of Jonah which I had adapted from Boko. These books had quite a few mistakes understandably, but we later revised them with our language informants, so that we could give them more accurate copies next time.

We decided that we should work on a third language called Busa. This one was easier for us, because it was a dialect of Boko. One Busa village called Sambe had a church, but no pastor, so I requested the Boko church to look for a suitable pastor to send there. It was time for the Boko church to develop their own missionary program. They had a mission-field close by, just over the border in Nigeria. It was not easy for Levi and I to evangelize these Muslim groups. We had been welcomed as language researchers and literacy workers, but if the locals felt we were trying to convert them, they would disappear like the evening shadows. So, we encouraged others to come in and build on the foundation we were laying.

In 2012 I appointed men to the Kyanga, Shanga and Busa translation teams. Except for Kyanga, where we had two Christians on the team, all the others were Muslims who had been working with me for two or three years on language research. Until this time, I had been staying at the Baptist church at Lolo, but as the Muslims didn't feel comfortable working at a church, I moved my base to a Kyanga village called Tungan Bage. Some Nigerian missionaries were based there, but their household just looked like any other household, and it was on the edge of the town. It was only a few miles from the Benin Republic border.

The plan was for all three teams to work together, so they could learn from each other's languages and how the others expressed things. The grammar and vocabularies of the languages were similar, but they couldn't understand each other. A five-year translation project was drawn up with a budget of AU$190,000. During that time, we were able to give these three endangered languages thirty-six percent of the Bible, seventy percent of the New Testament and twenty-five percent of the Old Testament. I travelled to Nigeria twice a year for six-week workshops. I linked up with the SIL related group, The Seed Company, who took financial responsibility for half of the project and helped me to get my Nigerian residence permit. SIM Nigeria was my sponsor, and SIM Australia handled the finances.

The Seed Company began in 1993 with a mandate to accelerate Bible translation. It started with pilot projects in ten different languages linked to prayer partners and investors. They train nationals to do the translation rather than sending in foreign missionaries. Missionaries initiated and led the modern Bible translation movement in the mid-20th century. By the 1980's however, they realized that it would take 150 years at the current rate of translation to reach every people group. By 2002 The Seed Company reached its two-hundredth language group, all projects being led by national translators. By 2017 the number was 1466. They hope to start projects in all unreached languages by the year 2025.

It was a friend, David Cummings, who suggested the Seed Company to me. My initial contacts with them were negative, because Westerners usually only work in these projects as consultants, but then I was directed to Dr Katy Barnwell. She had worked with SIL in Nigeria for many years and she had taught me grammar back in 1968 at an SIL linguistics course in UK. She thought I would be admirably suited to the Seed Company, working as both translator and consultant for the three languages.

The Shanga workers had to travel 160 miles to Tungan Bage and as they were teachers, I had to organize my trips for times when they were on holiday. Because my language informants were Muslims, we started with OT books like Genesis, Proverbs, and Jonah. I did the adaptations from Boko into the three languages while in Australia, then we worked on them together during my six-week field trips.

Travel in Nigeria is never easy. One year I was being driven five-hundred miles from Jos to Yauri. The trip took ten hours and we stopped about forty times at police and military checkpoints. It was actually reassuring to see the security forces on the road, and they didn't hold us up at all. They greeted us with comments like, "Good morning", "Well done!", "Where from?", "How family?". Only once was I asked, "What's in bag?"

Kyanga team translating John's Gospel

I was hesitant about translating John's Gospel with the teams. Were they ready to hear Jesus' claim to be one with the Father? I needn't have worried. After translating John 8 in Kyanga, one member named Musa said: "Ross has come to bring us light." However, we sometimes had problems with the Muslim workers. One day when the Shanga men saw a chicken being slaughtered for our dinner, they said they would not be able to eat it, because they saw it was slaughtered by Christians, and therefore not *halal*. In fact, the Quran says that Christian food is OK to eat, but most Muslims can't read the Quran and live according to what they are told in the mosque.

The outreach among the Kyanga being carried on by the CAPRO missionaries was very slow. Under Sharia law you have to be very careful who you talk to. The early Christian converts had been ostracized to such an extent that they all reverted to Islam. But just three miles away, at a village called Tungan Noma in Benin Republic, there is no Sharia law, and things are more relaxed. Before I came on the scene some Christians went to Tungan Noma to record the Jesus film in Kyanga. One local man who helped out was Isaac. He became a Christian and decided to build a church for his family. This church was eventually connected to a Baptist missionary work in northern Benin. Isaac and his brother Abdulaye were members of my Kyanga translation team. The Baptists gave them some pastoral training and helped them build a larger church. There are now at least fifty worshippers there. Only one Busa village has a church, and Levi's son John is the pastor there.

I was never worried about security in Nigeria. Nigeria can be a pretty dangerous place, but the areas where I lived were not too bad. The fact that I always lived close to the indigenes was a bonus. And being able to speak a local language, Boko, helps. When you speak a local language, people tend to regard you as one of them.

Boko Haram means Western education is forbidden, *haram* the opposite of *halal*, which means permitted. It is a jihadist organization based in the northeast of Nigeria, Cameroon and Niger, which strongly opposes westernization. The organization wants to establish Sharia law in all of Nigeria, and eventually make Nigeria an Islamic state. They are known for attacking Sufis and Christians and for bombing churches. Boko Haram have been responsible for tens of thousands of killings in West Africa since its founding in 2001.

When I lived at Tungan Bage, I had no cause to fear the local people. They appreciated the humanitarian work done by the missionaries. And the village head appreciated our presence there. But every now and then some aggressive Muslims would pass through and question why missionaries should be allowed to live in the area. One of the Muslim leaders spent a lot of time at our household, and the suspicion was that he was spying on us. He tried to make trouble for us on a couple of occasions. I heard reports of a mosque preacher in the State capital, who spoke of a dangerous Dr Ross, who was converting everyone to Christianity. And a local Iman had been warning people that we were translating the Bible so that their children and grandchildren would end up becoming Christians. In a team meeting on our base, it was suggested that I should not be seen as being active in evangelism. A white man in the north of Nigeria is very conspicuous, so I should stick to my official job description as "community worker specializing in language development, translation work and literacy".

In 2014 I decided to build a more comfortable house at Tungan Bage, so that I could spend more time there. By comfortable I mean a proper bed, a small refrigerator, a TV and an AC for the hotter months. I would also need to have solar panels, a converter, and batteries to supply power. Jolly, the CAPRO missionary at Tungan Bage, was excited and got someone to build the house straight away for AU$5,400.

After visiting Paul and family in UK, I flew to Jos and bought some second-hand furniture, the solar panels, frig, fan, generator etc. and a small bus carried it all to Lolo, fourteen miles from Tungan Bage. The final track had some steep ravines, so a pick-up truck made two trips to take my loads there. Two electricians accompanied us, so that they could install the solar panels and connect the other houses on the compound to it. Wow! We now had light and power twenty-four hours a day. What a difference that made.

I had come for four months and was now going home for Christmas for six weeks before returning. But then I decided I had better stay home in Australia for six months. Firstly, the daily temperature at Tungan Bage from mid-February to May was 40-45 degrees, and secondly there was a lot of work that I had to do making adaptations and working on the dictionaries that I could better do by myself. In addition, I was sure my AC unit was not going to cope. So, in 2014 and 2015 I spent six months each year at Tungan Bage and we were able to finish the translation work and the five-thousand-word dictionaries in Kyanga, Shanga and Busa.

Our word for Lord in Busa was literally 'slave owner'. It sounded too despotic. It seemed that the Busa had no word meaning 'lord, master, boss', except 'big man', and that was not suitable. Then when we translated Isaiah 1:3, "the ox knows its master", they came up with a new word for master, "deke", meaning 'owner'. After testing, we found it suitable for translating Lord. We also changed the Shanga word for Lord from 'Giver' to 'Householder', or 'Lord of the manor'.

With hostel manager Sanusi

In 2013 I met an eighteen-year old Christian Kyanga boy from Benin, named Sanusi, and I hired him as a cook. There were usually four-to-ten people each day to cook for and Sanusi proved to be a very good worker. He also pumped the water from the well, washed clothes, and swept the house. Believers from Benin can be open about their faith, but in Nigeria there are ten secret believers. Some of them have been baptized in the darkness of midnight. One of them used to visit me, and one day he brought a friend he was witnessing to. His in-laws were threatening to take his wife from him because of his faith. Life is extremely difficult for the first converts. I heard that some ECWA missionaries had several prayer stations and some converts among the Shanga, which was very encouraging, but I was not able to confirm it.

An American mission called Faith Comes by Hearing came and recorded the three New Testament translations we had done. They also recorded the Boko, Bokobaru and Bisā New Testaments for us. We bought some foam mattresses to make three studios where the recordings were made, and the solar panels worked well enough for them. The following year SIL Media from Jos came and recorded the OT portions we had translated. Then SIL Media recorded the Old Testament books for all six languages and transferred all the recordings onto five-hundred MP3 players I bought in Canada, together with some Boko music. These have been distributed among the various language groups by pastors and missionaries that are working there. These recordings are also available on the internet. My work at Tungan Bage finished in August 2016 and my last translation project officially finished on December 31st, 2017.

Approaching Eighty

2017- ?

Students at the hostel in Parakou

In 2017 and 2018 I made two-month trips to Benin during July and August to escape the Melbourne winter and enjoy the Benin rainy season. Over four-thousand booklets were photocopied and sent to workers for distribution in the various languages in Benin and Nigeria. The audio recordings of the Bible translations were completed and transferred to five-hundred MP3 players which were also sent out for distribution. An unexpected bonus came when a missionary in Burkina Faso offered to make phone applications of all my translations. They cost nothing and anyone who has a smartphone can download them for free from the internet. Every Boko, Bokobaru, Bisã, Busa, Kyanga and Shanga person now has the opportunity to have the Scriptures we have translated in his/her own phone. And they can download another application called Bible. is and access the audio recordings of these languages. One third of Boko Christians have mobile phones, but currently only ten-percent have smartphones. In addition, the videos of Luke's gospel recorded 20 years ago in Boko, Bokobaru and Bisã were redone with better color and sound and are available on CD.

In 2017 I rented a large house near the university in Parakou to accommodate twenty Christian university students from the north of Benin. Most of them are Boko, the first generation of university students. I pay for their accommodation and I pay the power and water bills. They are responsible for food, transport, fees, etc. If they fail a year, they must leave to give others a chance, and they must leave when they finish their first degree. They also receive an annual grant of AU$200 each to help with expenses, as do a few more who attend the university in Cotonou. Sanusi is the very capable manager, he is hard working and honest and he organizes a Bible study there each week. He pays the bills and fixes the taps and keeps the place running smoothly. He has been a great friend for me in the past few years. On my trips to Benin, he stays with me and cooks for me and my workers, usually four to six people. I paid his way through his degree course in English and now he has started a Masters in Project Development.

On Christmas day 2017 my whole family had a lovely reunion at my home in Wheelers Hill. The last get-together was for my seventieth birthday in 2010. Five grandchildren had been added since then. Peter's wife Sallie has been leading an effort to help dairy farmers in Gippsland. She launched a gourmet milk brand called Gippsland Jersey. A percentage of the profits goes toward helping farmers suffering from depression. Sallie is very capable, has a great business mind, and is a wonderful communicator. She started a farmer's market in Warragul and then a farmer's market for kids. Her work in raising awareness of the mental health of farmers was recognized by the government, and she was appointed to the national mental health board. She was also given a free trip to China with a delegation of entrepreneurial women.

Sal & Pete, Naomi & Andrew, Noah, Ross, Paul, Matt, Max, Mali, Katy with Eden, Sofi, Ros, Tessa, Evie, Billy, Reuben, Hudson (Christmas 2017)

When visiting Segbana I met a young man named Abu. His father died when he was an infant, and he was adopted into a Muslim family. Following the beliefs of his traditional religion, he used to

231

travel to Lugu each year to make a sacrifice to Tãasia, his personal spirit. He would take a chicken and go to the priest responsible for Tãasia. The priest would kill the chicken, spatter the blood and some feathers, and invoke the spirit, asking for his blessing on Abu. The priest was rewarded with the chicken's legs, while Abu would eat some and give the rest to children.

When in his twenties, Abu started having fevers and sleeplessness at night. He wasn't well at all and had to stop making his yearly pilgrimage to Tãasia. He thought that his ancestors weren't happy with him and that was the reason why he was sick. Then he started having dreams about black animals, pigs and donkeys, and often saw himself being pursued by his stepfather. One day when going to the village of Kolowi, he met a dog on the road, which made his hair stand on end. He believed it was possessed. His stepfather had joined a group of sorcerers in the hope that he would become rich. This often required giving a member of the family as a sacrifice. Abu became convinced that he was the victim, and that was why he was always sick and having bad dreams. He left his adopted home and rented a room.

Abu visited a Christian friend, named Jacob, and told him about his problem. Jacob took him to church and introduced him to the pastor. The pastor and some elders of the church prayed for Abu for several Sundays until he felt completely healed, then Abu surrendered his life to Jesus Christ as his Lord and Savior. He was baptized, and after witnessing to five Muslim friends from Kolowi, they also became Christians. Kolowi was the first village that Bob Blaschke preached in sixty years previously, and the first Boko church was formed from converts from this village. But most of the village, including the Christians, had moved into Segbana to live, while the others chose to stay in their old village. As a result of Abu's witness, there is now a group of thirty believers there and they have recently built a church.

Levi's son John began a project for me among the Kyanga, Shanga and Busa in 2015 with sixty Busa farmers. They all received $100 microloans and training, that enabled many of them to double the size of their crops. In 2016 he trained 120 Busa and sixty Kyanga. In 2017 and 2018 he trained 180 Kyanga from four villages. The recipients are all Muslim and we pray that they will appreciate the Christian aid and that some will respond. In 2020 he hopes to move to the Shanga area and do more of the same.

During these last few years in Australia my life has revolved around three areas: family, Indian students and writing books. Three of my sons and my sister, Libby, live less than an hour's drive away and I visit them for an evening meal every two or three weeks. They are all very busy and it is easier for me to visit them than vice versa. I appreciate the meals away from home. A widower's life could be a very lonely one, especially if there are no family members nearby. My life is kept busy by having a household full of Indian student boarders, sometimes in the double figures! I buy all the food and am able to keep the food bills down to $100 a month per head. I enjoy their curries and play tennis with a few of the boys. We also have occasional outings to the sea on the Mornington Peninsula.

I have always loved reading books. In the first decade of my life it was comics, mainly Archie comics. In the second decade it was Biggles books. In the third it was missionary biographies, and in the fourth it was Agatha Christie detective novels; I needed some light reading there in the African bush. During the last fifty years as a Bible translator I have been continually delving into commentaries on different books of the Bible book and studying the meaning of words in Greek and Hebrew dictionaries. In later years I have read extensively on creation and evolution and come down strongly in favor of creation. After all, I am a Bible translator and I believe the Biblical record. I also enjoy reading books about physicists and their understanding of the structure of the atom and the quantum theory. Those, mainly Jewish, intellectuals are truly geniuses. I feel sorry for people who haven't got into the practice of reading; they miss out on so much.

For twenty years I have had the desire to write a book about my understanding of the Kingdom of God that Jesus spoke about so often, but I never had the time. In 2011 I spent a month writing down memoirs of my life as a missionary, and they have been sitting in my computer ever since. So, after my trip to Africa in 2017, I realized that my translation work was finally over and that I now had time to write my books. A third book, a commentary on the book of Revelation developed from my book on the Kingdom of God. The three books will be published by Xlibris before the end of 2019. The titles are: The Kingdom from God – unlocking the secrets, Apocalyptic Terror and Millennial Glory, and the biography: Aspires to Lofty Heights.

Joy always used to say, "Jonesy always lands on his feet." Or, as expressed by the apostle Paul, "And we know that in all things God works for the good of those who love him, who have been called according to his purpose." (Romans 8:28). I continually praise God for his goodness towards me; for drawing me to himself and saving me, for giving me his peace and joy and courage to aspire to lofty heights. My second name McCallum is my maternal grandmother's maiden name, and that is the McCallum family motto In arduo tendit means "aspires to lofty heights" or "attempts difficult things".

I have loved my life and God has been so faithful to me. The 9th July 2019 was the fiftieth anniversary of my arrival in Benin. There have been the difficult times, but my optimism and faith in God have always carried me through. I would never have chosen to be a Bible translator, linguist or lexicographer, but that was what God chose for me, and he knows best. I just loved my work so much: analyzing grammar, translating the precious word of God into African languages, compiling dictionaries, evangelizing, teaching the word of God, building the Boko church, nurturing a lovely family in Benin and in Australia, encouraging students. It is great to have a purpose in life which is beyond money, houses and things. Jesus said, "No one who has left home or wife or brothers or sisters or parents or children for the sake of the kingdom of God will fail to receive many times as much in this age, and in the age to come eternal life" (Luke 18:29-30). I've received much back in return, and now I look forward to my glorification. Not this world's glory, but the glory of receiving an immortal, supernatural, resurrection body, of being revealed as a child of God, of reigning with Christ here on earth for one thousand years, and of living with God in the glorious New Jerusalem throughout eternity.

What do I have to look forward to from here on? In this life I'm not sure. Who knows tomorrow? But life in the next world is more certain. There "those who are wise will shine like the brightness of the heavens, and those who lead many to righteousness, like the stars for ever and ever" (Daniel 12:3). Those who have surrendered their lives to God have hope that they will be included in that number. As it is written on the last page of the Bible:

They will see his face, and his name will be on their foreheads. There will be no more night. They will not need the light of a lamp or the light of the sun, for the Lord God will give them light. And they will reign for ever and ever (Revelation 22:4-5).

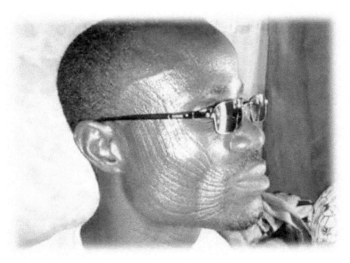

Kyanga facial marking